AURA GARDEN GUIDES

Karlheinz Jacobi

Roses

AURA BOOKS

Aura Garden Guides

Roses
Karlheinz Jacobi

Original German language edition:
Gärten leicht und richtig
Rosen
© 1992 BLV Verlagsgesellschaft
mbH, München, Germany

This edition produced by:
Transedition Limited for
Aura Books, Bicester
and first published in 2002

English language edition
© 1995 Advanced Marketing (UK) Ltd.,
Bicester, England

English language translation by:
Andrew Shackleton for Translate-A-Book,
a division of Transedition Ltd.,
Oxford

Typesetting by:
Organ Graphic, Abingdon

10 9 8 7 6 5 4 3 2
Printed in Dubai

ISBN 1 901683 89 3

Photographic credits
AKG, Berlin 88, 89; Apel 13 centre
right, 16 bottom, 39, 51, 54, 55;
Burda 90, 91; CMA 32/33, 92/93;
Eigstler 5, 11 centre, 12/13, 27 centre
right, 61, backcover right; Henseler
73; Hoppe 40/41, 43, 50 bottom,
78/79, 94/95; Jensen, Glücksburg 52;
J. S. Mattock 7 bottom, 8 top, 12
centre left, 14, 16/17, 21 right, 22, 23
top and bottom, 25, 27 bottom, 35
top centre, 40, 66/67, 75 top, 80/81;
Morell 9 top, 10/11, 34, 37, 49, 50
top, 75 centre right, backcover left;
Niehoff 57; Photos Horticultural
frontcover; Redeleit 45, 58, 66, 67,
79; Reinhard 8 centre left and
bottom, 9 centre right, 11 right, 18,
19, 21 top left, 23 centre right, 24, 26
centre left, 27 top, 28, 29, 31, 35 top
left and centre right, 36/37, 38, 41,
46/47, 48, 59, 64, 65 top, 75 bottom,
83; Rosen Tantau, Uetersen 56; Rosen
Union, Bad Nauheim-Steinfurth 12
bottom left, 13 bottom; Ruckszio 9
bottom, 15 centre right, 26 bottom,
74 centre left, 76 top, 84, 86; Sammer
2, 7 top and centre right, 15 bottom,
18/19, 35 bottom right, 53, 62, 63,
72, 76 bottom left and bottom right,
87, 92; Seidl 6, 12 top left, 13 top
right, 20/21, 30, 65 bottom, 68/69, 74
bottom; Schlüter 77, 78 left; Strobel,
Pinneberg 44

CONTENTS

A summary

Everyone should have some roses in their garden. Two things make them an almost essential feature: their flowers, which provide delightful scents and colours for many months of the year, and their sheer versatility. Bush roses, for example, can turn whole areas of the garden into a sea of colour: climbing roses can be used to cover walls and pergolas, and wild roses are ideal for making an impenetrable hedge. Shrub roses can be used either alone or in combination with other shrubs as an eye-catching centrepiece for the garden.

Even if you live in a flat, or don't have a garden, you can still grow miniature roses in window boxes and pots. And ground-covering roses are just about the most pleasant and environmentally friendly way to suppress weeds in a flower bed. The most popular roses, and those with the largest number of varieties, are the hybrid teas; but there are many other classes of rose that are equally beautiful, and new cultivars are appearing every year.

The dividing lines between these classes aren't always very clear, and can be the subject of occasional disagreement. The following is the most widely accepted classification.

Bush, or bedding roses are roses of medium height, ranging between about 16 and 40 in (40–100 cm). They can be divided into two main categories: hybrid teas and floribundas. Hybrid teas have many blooms (which are often fragrant) and petals that form a distinctive raised cone shape. They are less bushy than floribundas, and usually have only one flower to each stem. Hybrid teas tend to flower in flushes, rather than continuously. These are the most popular roses, and the most usual choice for cut flowers and for exhibition. The most distinctive feature of floribundas is that the flowers grow in clusters rather than individually. The blooms tend to be smaller and less elegant than those of hybrid teas, but they have the big advantage of appearing recurrently through the summer and autumn and providing a more prominent splash of colour.

Shrub roses go particularly well with other ornamental shrubs. They are taller than the more common bush roses, reaching a maximum height and spread of 10–13 ft (3–4 m). Rose experts often distinguish between recurrent shrub roses (which are more popular because they flower repeatedly throughout the season) and non-recurrent shrub roses (which flower only once a year). All shrub roses are very hardy; they don't need regular pruning and bear attractive hips in autumn.

Climbing and rambling roses have long, climbing stems which must be tied onto a support such as a trellis, pergola, fence or wall. Rambling varieties reach a height of around 20 ft (6 m), and flower only once a year. Climbing roses are smaller, at around 13 ft (4 m), with less flexible stems; many flower repeatedly each summer.

Patio and miniature roses come in many varieties, most of them only around 12 in (30 cm) high. They are repeat-flowering, and their small flowers and attractive leaves make them ideal for window boxes and other containers.

Ground-cover roses are a group of low-growing roses that can be used to provide lasting ground cover in a flower bed. They vary in height from about 8 to 32 in (20–80 cm), with a prostrate growth habit, forming small clumps or arching stems.

Standard roses are hybrid tea, floribunda, patio, miniature or rambling roses budded onto rootstocks up to 56 in (140 cm) high. The tallest and most dramatic are weeping standards, which use the pliable stems of rambling rose varieties to achieve cascades of colour. Standards are a way of growing roses rather than a specific class of rose.

Nearly all types of rose will grow best in a sunny position.

Floribundas

Floribunda roses have many different uses in the garden. They can provide a lighter contrast with the dark green leaves of conifers, or create colour between ornamental shrubs that have finished flowering. They can be grown in containers or as low-growing hedges, and can look particularly striking if they're grown in combination with herbaceous perennials. But all floribundas look their best when grown in quantity — in rows, groups or whole beds of one colour or variety.

You can exploit the fact that different varieties grow to different heights by placing taller roses and standards at the back of the border or at the centre of the bed. Floribundas range in height from about 10 to 60 in (25-150 cm): this depends not only on the variety, but also on their position in the garden, how well they are looked after, and the prevailing local climate.

Floribundas should be planted about 18-36 in (45-90 cm) apart; if they're planted in groups, there should be one to five roses per square yard/

metre. Although they aren't as tall as shrub roses, and don't spread out as far, some floribundas may grow as high as shrub roses if given little or no pruning.

Floribundas vary enormously in flower size, number of petals, and fragrance: some have no fragrance at all, while are so strongly scented that they're impossible to ignore. Traditionally they've been regarded as second best to hybrid teas; certainly they tend to be less elegant. But breeding has helped to remove some of their limitations, and some varieties are indistinguishable from hybrid teas.

Because there's such an enormous range of varieties, and they come in so many different colours, the list of floribundas below is arranged according to colour to make your choice easier.

The floribunda 'Rumba', planted with ornamental grasses and catmint

Red varieties

Variety	Colour	Height in inches (cm)	Remarks
'Chorus'	bright red	20–28 (50–70)	large, full double flowers, mildew-resistant, tolerates semi-shade
'Lili Marlene'	dark crimson	20–28 (50–70)	large, moderately full double flowers; very attractive, tolerates semi-shade
'Mother's Day'	scarlet	12–20 (30–50)	small double flowers, low-growing, suitable for containers
'Beautiful Britain'	tomato red	28–48 (70–120)	medium-sized double blooms with a light scent
'City of Birmingham'	crimson scarlet	40–60 (100–150)	large clusters of double blooms
'Frensham'	deep crimson	48–80 (120–200)	an old favourite with the vigour to make a good shrub
'Intrigue'	crimson velvet	40–48 (100–120)	very dark medium-sized blooms in big clusters
'The Times Rose'	crimson scarlet	32–48 (80–120)	the healthiest dark red floribunda with deep green foliage

'Lili Marlene'

'Glad Tidings'
'The Times Rose'

7

'Trumpeter'

Orange varieties

Variety	Colour	Height in inches (cm)	Remarks
'Orange Sensation'	light vermilion	16-24 (40-60)	moderately full flowers, fragrant petals, vigorous
'Evelyn Fison'	bright vermilion	40-60 (100-150)	large trusses of medium-sized bright blooms
'Melody Maker'	light vermilion	32-48 (80-120)	perfectly shaped blooms, good for cutting
'Memento'	salmon red	32-48 (80-120)	very profuse, with long stems for cutting
'Trumpeter'	vermilion orange	30-40 (75-100)	the perfect short-growing bedding rose

'Korresia'

'Helga'

Yellow varieties

Variety	Colour	Height in inches (cm)	Remarks
'Allgold'	buttercup yellow	20-28 (50-70)	semi-double, disease-resistant
'Honey Bunch'	honey yellow	16-24 (40-60)	fully double, good for cutting
'Korresia'	bright golden yellow	16-24 (40-60)	full double flowers, vigorous, good for cutting
'Mountbatten'	clear yellow	40-60 (100-150)	large double blooms on a vigorous plant

White and cream varieties

Variety	Colour	Height in inches (cm)	Remarks
'Helga'	pure white	24-32 (60-80)	moderately full, very large flowers, very free-flowering
'Margaret Merril'	white and delicate yellowish pink	16-24 (40-60)	very fragrant, semi-double to double flowers
'Snowline'	creamy white	16-24 (40-60)	moderately full
'Iceberg'	pure white	40-80 (100-200)	vigorous, free flowering, repeats frequently

Pink varieties

Variety	Colour	Height in inches (cm)	Remarks
'Anisley Dickson'	salmon pink	16-24 (40-60)	moderately full flowers
'Bonica 82'	light pink	16-24 (40-60)	medium-sized, very full flowers
'Sweet Promise'	salmon pink	20-28 (50-70)	large, slightly fragrant flowers
'The Queen Elizabeth Rose'	light pink	32-40 (80-100)	large, hybrid-tea-like full flowers, tolerates semi-shade
'Anna Livia'	pink	36-52 (90-130)	perfectly shaped blooms in clusters

'Bonica'

Varieties with unusual colours/more than one colour

Variety	Colour	Height in inches (cm)	Remarks
'Greensleeves'	pink changing to green	20-28 (50-70)	good cut flower
'International Herald Tribune'	violet with yellow centre	12-20 (30-50)	fragrant, free-flowering
'Shocking Blue'	lilac	20-28 (50-70)	very fragrant, good for cutting, free-flowering
'Brown Velvet'	russet brown	36-44 (90-110)	a good variety for flower arrangers
'Christopher Columbus'	pale pink striped red	30-40 (75-100)	a completely novel colour with good clusters
'Hannah Gordon'	white with a cherry-pink edge	40-48 (100-120)	beautifully shaped flowers
'Intrigue'	very dark crimson	16-24 (40-60)	moderately full, very hardy
'Matangi'	orange vermilion blend	36-48 (90-120)	very free-flowering, tidy plant with a novel colour
'Tango'	orange with pale yellow	40-60 (100-150)	a bushy plant that will grow into a shrub

'Shocking Blue'

'Intrigue'

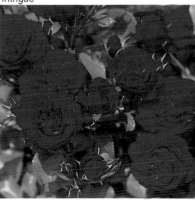

Hybrid teas

Where to plant hybrid teas

These roses are officially classed as large-flowered bush roses. However, they're better known under their traditional name — hybrid teas — and are arguably the most beautiful of all roses. They have large, often scented flowers with a high centre, and usually they have large numbers of petals.

Hybrid teas come in a wide variety of colours ranging from pure white through yellow, pink and orange to red. There's also plenty of choice for lovers of unusual colours: you can have bronze, copper or lilac hybrid teas, as well as roses in two or more different colours. The number of varieties is so huge that there's really no substitute for visiting a specialist rose grower or rose garden and seeing them for yourself. This is the best way to choose roses, particularly as the colours shown in some nursery catalogues may not actually be very true to life.

Most hybrid teas are relatively straight-stemmed and upright-growing. Most are bushy to a greater or lesser extent, and vary in height between 20 and 40 in (50–100 cm) or more. 'Peace', for example, is a very well-known variety which forms bushes growing up to 64 in (160 cm) high.

Generally speaking, hybrid teas are less bushy than floribunda roses, and the classic

hybrid teas such as 'Selfridges' have a single flower on the end of a straight stem, making them ideal for cutting. The newer varieties have narrow, elegant flowers with the central petals in a distinctive spiral shape. In some hybrid teas, such as the beautifully fragrant 'Just Joey', the flowers form a bowl shape when they are past their best.

A striking but restrained combination of colours: hybrid tea 'Elina' and sage

The delicate beauty of hybrid teas means they should be planted in a very sheltered place, and will need more care than other roses. Unlike floribunda, shrub and climbing roses, they're best planted in groups of different varieties in a specific rose bed. Ideally, this should be dug in a place where the roses can be viewed at leisure from a position close by — on a patio or near a garden bench for example.

The rose expert Alma d'Aigle produced a unique classification of rose fragrances which is still in use today. Her views on

colour harmonies are also well worth noting. 'It is hard to go wrong if the colours of hybrid teas are properly matched. Whether one plants beds or rows of the same variety, whether one plants irregular groups of a single colour, or mixes red with pink, yellow with orange, and crimson with white: their natural nobility is evidenced by the fact that each stands alone in its beauty and does not strive to outdo its neighbours. A group of hybrid tea roses must be like a circle of friends in which each is different, each is a personality in itself, wholly unpretentious, with none subordinate to another.'

Single, semi-double and double flowers

There are many different ways of classifying roses: they may be grouped by variety, by their growth habit, by the colour, size and shape of their flowers, or finally by the number of petals.

Depending on the number of petals in each flower, the rose is classified as single, semi-double or double. Single-flowered roses (e.g. the wild roses) rarely have more than five petals. One example is the Golden Rose of China, *Rosa hugonis*. Semi-double roses have between eight and twenty petals; the most attractive examples include many of the shrub rose varieties, some of which are spring-flowering. Double-flowered roses include many hybrid teas, ground-covering roses, miniature and climbing roses. These have from 20 to 35 petals, and sometimes more. They are nearly all hybrid teas, though they also include shrub, floribunda and climbing roses. As their name suggests, the centifolia roses have around a hundred petals! Their only rivals in this respect are some of the 'New English' roses such as 'English Garden', 'Graham Thomas' and 'L. D. Braithwaite'.

Even single-flowered roses can be very beautiful.

A very full double rose, 'Königin von Dänemark'

'Super Star'

'Silver Jubilee'

'Julia's Rose'

A selection of particularly good hybrid teas for the garden

White flowers: 'Elina', 'Evening Star', 'Pascali', 'Polar Star', 'Virgo'

Orange: 'Beautè', golden apricot; 'Colour Wonder', salmon orange; 'Just Joey', copper; 'Lovers Meeting', tangerine; 'Rebecca Claire', coppery orange; 'Remember Me', rich coppery orange; 'Troika', orange bronze, 'Valencia', pure apricot.

Yellow: 'Freedom', unfading yellow; 'Grandpa Dickson', lemon yellow; 'King's Ransom', golden yellow; 'Peer Gynt', yellow and peach; 'Selfridges', bright yellow; 'Simba', clear yellow; 'Sunblest', pure yellow; 'Sutter's Gold', golden yellow; 'Whisky Mac', bronze yellow.

12

'Sutter's Gold'

'Peace'

'Ingrid Bergman'

Pink: 'Blessings', coral pink; 'Congratulations', bright pink; 'Fragrant Hour', salmon pink; 'Keepsake', bright old pink; 'The Macartney Rose', glowing pink; 'Margaret', silvery-pink; 'Margaret Thatcher', porcelain pink; 'Paul Sherville', salmon pink; 'Savoy Hotel', pastel pink; 'Silver Jubilee', salmon pink.

Red: 'Alec's Red', deep red; 'Alexander', vermilion; 'Ena Harkness', scarlet; 'Fragrant Cloud', coral red; 'Ingrid Bergmann', dark red; 'Loving Memory', crimson–scarlet; 'Malcolm Sargent', dark red; 'National Trust', ruby red; 'Royal William', crimson velvet.

Unusual colours: 'Blue Moon', lilac; 'Julia's Rose', parchment-coloured; 'Mary Pope', fuchsia purple.

'Kordes' Robusta'

'Miss Pam Ayres'

Repeat-flowering shrub roses

All roses are actually shrubs, but shrub roses differ from hybrid teas and floribundas in their more vigorous growth. Some of these ornamental shrub roses can grow to a height and spread of 10-13 ft (3-4 m) in the right conditions.

Ideally, these roses should be planted so they can be admired from all sides. They look good if grown as specimen plants in an

Repeat-flowering shrub roses

Variety	Habit	Height in inches (cm)	Remarks
'Fountain'	broad, bushy, medium height, upright growth habit	52-60 (130-150)	large, hybrid-tea-like, slightly fragrant dark-red flowers
'Kordes' Robusta'	stiff, upright growth habit	60-80 (150-200)	medium-sized, single blood-red flowers with golden filaments, very long flowering period, very thorny; good for hedges (plant 20 in/ 50 cm apart)
'Westerland'	upright, very spreading habit	60-80 (150-200)	large, very fragrant yellowish-orange flowers
'Radox Bouquet'	vigorous	32-48 (80-120)	flowers large, very full, pure pink, highly fragrant; makes a good unpruned hedge (plant 30 in/75 cm apart)
'Ballerina'	extremely free-growing short shrub, useful as an ornamental hedge	40-60 (100-150)	a pretty plant with large pink and white flower clusters, reminiscent of phlox
'Jacqueline du Pré'	nicely rounded shrub with dark, shiny foliage	40-60 (100-150)	the pure-white flowers have a good scent and begin producing colour early in the season

Repeat-flowering shrub roses

Variety	Habit	Height in inches (cm)	Remarks
'Golden Wings'	beautiful shrub with bright green, very healthy foliage	40–80 (100–200)	the large, single light-yellow blooms are spectacular, and have a slight scent
'Kathleen Ferrier'	a plant with an arching habit, an asset in any border	60–80 (150–200)	the medium-sized blooms of salmon pink are heavily scented
'Miss Pam Ayres'	upright plant well furnished with luxuriant medium green foliage	60–80 (150–200)	the clusters of bright yellow flowers turn red as they age
'Red Dot'	robust shrub with handsome dark green foliage	60–80 (150–200)	eye-catching clusters of pretty, bright-red blooms
'Yesterday'	this plant will develop into a low-growing shrub	40–60 (100–150)	the clusters of small, red magenta blooms have an old-world appearance, and are heavily scented
'Marjorie Fair'	often described as a red 'Ballerina': a lovely low-growing shrub	40–60 (100–150)	clusters of red blooms with a white eye, which are very weather resistant
'Angelina'	another nicely rounded shrub which will do equally well as a semi-climber	40–80 (100–200)	large, semi-double blooms delicately shaded peach

island bed surrounded by low-growing perennials, or set off against dark green conifers. In a small garden you will probably have room for only one, but they can look spectacular planted in threes. In a large garden, these shrub roses can also be made into a flowering, unpruned hedge, perhaps using varieties such as 'Golden Wings', 'Angelina' or 'Radox Bouquet'. You could also combine roses with another shrub, such as privet, to make a hedge. The beautiful colours of this very attractive class of roses range from white through yellow, pink and red to lilac.

'Westerland'

'Iceberg'

15

Summer-flowering shrub roses: modern shrub roses

The term 'modern shrub roses' refers to various types of rose with different origins. They are shrub-sized hybrids of wild roses, and have many different uses in the garden. Most are best grown on their own as specimen shrubs, while others make excellent hedges. Some also bear attractive hips in autumn. This often makes them popular with birds, both as a source of food and as a highly suitable nesting place.

The same is true of wild roses, which have been a feature of gardens for centuries. Wild roses are characterised by single flowers and widely varying growth habits.

Summer-flowering shrub roses have a stiff, upright growth habit; some have arching branches. Most flower very early in the year, in May and early June, with large numbers of single, semi-double or double flowers depending on the individual variety.

Nearly all shrub roses flower on old wood, with the flowering shoots growing from branches several years old. They should therefore be pruned only once every four to five years, after they have flowered, rather than annually like hybrid teas and floribundas. Prune old, crowded stems right down to ground level, and cut back long

Above *'Mme Isaac Pereire'*

Left *'Marguerite Hilling'*, a modern shrub rose

shoots to an outward-facing bud. Leave the flowers on the bush after they have faded, so that hips will form. The vigorous growth of these shrubs means they should be planted 40–60 in (100–150 cm) apart.

Modern summer-flowering shrub roses

Variety	Height in inches (cm)	Remarks
R. moyesii 'Marguerite Hilling'	60-80 (150-200)	large, semi-double pale pink flowers shaded with deep pink; goes well with perennials; plant 6 ft (2 m) apart
R. rugosa 'Conrad Ferdinand Meyer'	80-120 (200-300)	large, silvery-pink hybrid-tea-like flowers; early and very free-flowering; very fragrant; plant 60-100 in (150-250 cm) apart
R. rugosa 'Pink Grootendorst'	40-60 (100-150)	very thorny; small red flowers; plant 60-100 in (150-250 cm) apart
R. pimpinellifolia 'Frühlingsgold'	100-120 (250-300)	elegant arching stems; large single yellow, slightly fragrant flowers; flowers very freely in May; plant 6-10 ft (2-3 m) apart
R. multiflora 'Constance Spry'	60-80 (150-200)	large, sprawling shrub or climber; soft pink, lovely fragrant cupped blooms; flowers for about a month in midsummer; plant up to 60 in (150 cm) apart
R. canina 'Fritz Nobis'	60-80 (150-200)	salmon pink, semi double blooms with a good form; flowers in midsummer; plant 60 in (150 cm) apart
R. multibracteata 'Cerise Bouquet'	80-120 (200-300)	cerise crimson; grey foliage contributes to a spectacular plant; flowers towards end of high summer; plant 80 in (200 cm) apart
R. eglantaria 'Alchymist'	60-80 (150-200)	yellow shaded orange; a vigorous plant that can develop into a good climber; one of the earliest to flower; plant 60 in (150 cm) apart
R. gallica 'Scarlet Fire'	60-80 (150-200)	crimson scarlet; the large single blooms provide a stunning splash of colour mid-season; good harvest of hips in the autumn; plant 60 in (150 cm) apart

Summer-flowering shrub roses deserve a great deal more popularity. They shouldn't be regarded as second best, especially as they include many beautiful, old-fashioned varieties which recreate the charm of the traditional rose garden before hybridising began.

Other attractive summer-flowering modern shrub and moss roses include 'Nevada', 'Frühlingsmorgen', and 'F. J. Grootendorst'.

Climbing and rambling roses

Climbing and rambling roses are hardy, vigorous plants capable of growing stems several yards long. Like shrub roses, they flower on the side shoots rather than the main stem, so the more side shoots a climbing rose has, the more flowers it produces.

Summer-flowering climbers and ramblers come into bloom for up to a month each year, and repeat-flowering varieties often continue to flower until the first frosts.

Climbing and rambling roses are very versatile: they can be grown round doors and trellises, fences and steps; planted so that they grow high up into trees; or used to cover the walls of a house. They can be grown as a magnificent archway over a front gate, or to cover a pergola. They produce flowering stems up to 20 ft (6 m) long, or can be grown trailing. Climbers are ideal for hiding ugly views, and can even be grown on a balcony if you live in a flat.

Climbing roses can be grown on a north-facing wall, but they will produce fewer, paler-coloured flowers and are prone to pests such as spider mite — and other problems such as

balling. Climbers need to be tied onto a support of some kind, such as a trellis, rose arch, pergola or fence. Alternatively, you can simply attach them to lengths of plastic-covered wire stretched along a wall, or between posts or steel pipes. Train the main stems horizontally to create an even fan shape.

Climbing roses need more feeding than their non-climbing relatives, as they grow more new shoots each year. If you feed them regularly and generously, they will reward you with a longer flowering period and more flowers.

Top left *'Lavinia';* **top right** *'The New Dawn';* **right** *'Paul's Scarlet Climber'*

18

Climbing and rambling roses

Variety	Growth habit	Height in feet (m)	Remarks
'Golden Showers'	moderately vigorous, upright	7-10 (2-3)	large yellow semi-double flowers, long flowering period; needs sheltered position
'Heidelberg'	moderately vigorous, spreading, upright	7-10 (2-3)	large, double red flowers into late autumn
'Lavinia'	vigorous, bushy, upright	10-13 (3-4)	large pink double hybrid-tea-like flowers; long flowering period
'The New Dawn'	vigorous, spreading; arching stems	10-13 (3-4)	delicate pink, semi-double shell-pink flowers; very free-flowering, flowers until first frosts
'Paul's Scarlet Climber'	vigorous, bushy, upright	8-11 (2.5-3.5)	medium-sized, semi-double scarlet flowers shaded with crimson; only one flush of flowers, but very free-flowering
'Sympathie'	vigorous, upright	7-10 (2-3)	deep scarlet flowers, fragrant, repeat-flowering
'White Cockade'	moderately vigorous, upright	7 (2)	large white double flowers tinged with pink; fragrant, free-flowering and repeat-flowering
'Compassion'	moderately vigorous, will grow on any aspect	7-13 (2-4)	heavily scented, hybrid-tea-sized, salmon orange blooms all summer
'Dublin Bay'	usually matures to a height of 7 ft (2 m) but is slow-growing	7-10 (2-3)	moderate climber for the small garden, deep red flowers
'Mermaid'	if it likes your garden will easily grow to 30 ft (9 m) but is happiest in a warm position	7-20 (2-6)	famous single yellow with semi-evergreen foliage
'Schoolgirl'	a leggy climber	7-13 (2-4)	vigorous climber with large, fragrant copper orange flowers

Ground-cover roses

Ground-covering plants include low-growing, almost creeping shrubs such as cotoneasters and evergreen creeping juniper, and perennials such as creeping phlox, alyssum and candytuft. Their carpets of flowers, stems and leaves help to stop the soil drying out, and keep down weeds. There are a number of roses with a spreading growth habit which can be used for this purpose, combining beauty with practicality.

Ground-cover roses need just as much care as other types of rose. Old and dead stems need to be pruned each year, and grafted varieties are sometimes prone to suckers. These can be recognised by their pale green leaves, and should be cut off whenever they appear. Don't cut off upright shoots, as these will gradually arch over and create more ground cover. It's also important not to plant

these roses too close together (planting distances are included in the descriptions of individual varieties below). If you do, the shoots will be pushed upwards and the roses will lose their flat growth habit. When planting, it's also important to ensure that you carefully dig up all perennial weeds beforehand.

Some ground-cover roses have been around for a long time: the oldest is *Rosa × paulli*, which dates from 1903, and 'Max Graf' was introduced in 1919. Since then there have been so many varieties with different growth habits and colours that they're best divided into sub-groups.

A selection classified by growth habit

Non-vigorous, trailing:
'Nozomi': 8-12 in (20-30 cm) high; small, single, light pink flowers; 3-4 plants per sq yd/m; can also be used in rockeries and containers.

'Snow Carpet': 4-6 in (10-15 cm) high; very small, white, double flowers with a cream centre; 8-9 plants per sq yd/m; suitable for very small areas and rockeries.

Bushy:
'Moje Hammarberg': 28-32 in (70-80 cm) high, violet-pink, semi-double fragrant flowers and attractive hips; 2-3 plants per sq yd/m; also makes a good flowering hedge.

'Frau Dagmar Hartopp': 24-32 in (60-80 cm) high; medium-sized, single pink flowers; long flowering period, very large hips; 3-4 plants per sq yd/m; lime-hating.

Low-growing, bushy:
'Gwent': 30-40 in (75-100 cm) high and 40 in (100 cm) wide; a new double yellow prostrate form; 4 plants per sq yd/m.

'Suffolk': 20-30 in (50-75 cm) high and 40 in (100 cm) wide; large trusses of bright scarlet

> Ground-cover roses can be combined with dwarf conifers and other low-growing shrubs such as lavender, *Spiraea japonica*, deutzias and Rose of Sharon (*Hypericum calycinum*). Alternatively, grow them with perennials such as sedum, thyme and veronica.

'Swany'

Above *'Surrey'*
Left *'Max Graf'*

flowers followed by small, red hips; 3 plants per sq yd/m.

'Surrey': 30–40 in (75–100 cm) high and 40–48 in (100–120 cm) wide; soft pink double blooms with a slight fragrance; 3 plants per sq yd/m.

'Swany': vigorous, 16–20 in (40–50 cm) high, small to medium-sized salmon-pink flowers with white edges; free-flowering, with long flowering period; 3–4 plants per sq yd/m, 20–24 in (50–60 cm) apart.

Slightly arching.

'Ferdy': 40 in (100 cm) high and 40–60 in (100–150 cm) wide; soft fuchsia-pink double flowers on a beautiful arching shrub; 1–2 plants per sq yd/m.

'Smarty': 60 in (150 cm) high, creeping stems; large yellowish white flowers tinged with pink; slightly fragrant. Plant 28–40 in (70–100 cm) apart, or one to two plants per sq yd/m.

Prostrate, vigorous:

'Partridge': single, white to light pink flowers, rain-resistant; 3 ft (1 m) apart or 1–2 plants per sq yd/m.

'Max Graf': produces a dense mat. Around 12–16 in (30–40 cm) high if planted well apart (3 ft/1 m), but much taller (3–10 ft/1–3 m) if planted too close together (20–24 in/50–60 cm apart). Single crimson flowers in midsummer. 1–2 plants per sq yd/m; also suitable for low-growing hedges.

21

Miniature and patio roses

In many gardens, tall trees and bushes leave little room for sun-loving plants like roses. Of course there are some flori-bundas which tolerate semi-shade, but by far the majority of roses need full sun. Even so, there's no reason why you should have to do without roses in a shady garden. One option is to plant climbing roses, whose long stems grow upwards towards the light. The other possibility is miniature and patio roses, which have not always had the recognition they deserve from amateur gardeners. These vary in height from about 8 to 32 in (20–40 cm) depending on variety; most are very free-flowering, and can be grown in a window box, a large terracotta pot or some other container.

However, miniature and patio roses should be more than an afterthought used to fill a gap in the bed: they're an essential feature of the garden. They look particularly good in a rockery, where they act as an attractive stopgap in summer when carpeting perennials aren't flowering. They can also be used as an elegant edging plant for any kind of flower bed. If they're planted alongside a path, no one will ever dare to stray off it!

Plant miniature and patio roses about 10 in (25 cm) apart, or 12 plants to the square yard/metre. Nearly all of them are very resistant to disease and particularly hardy, producing large numbers of flowers over a long period.

'Gentle Touch'

Miniature and patio roses

Variety	Colour	Height in inches (cm)	Remarks
'Snowball'	white	4–12 (10–30)	small, fragrant double flowers; slightly arching habit; vigorous, disease-resistant
'Baby Masquerade'	yellow changing to red	8–16 (20–40)	free-flowering, bushy
'Blue Peter'	lilac–violet	8–16 (20–40)	large, semi-double flowers, bushy
'Orange Sunblaze' (other name: 'Sunblaze')	orange-red	12–16 (30–40)	large, full double flowers; moderately vigorous, very bushy
'Perestroika'	golden yellow	12–14 (30–35)	double flowers, bushy
'Angela Rippon'	glowing salmon	16 (40)	bushy grower with small double flowers
'Baby Sunrise'	orange and yellow	12 (30)	perfect little blooms; good as a pot plant
'Green Diamond'	greenish white	12 (30)	compact grower with small double blooms; a novelty
'Mandarin'	deep pink with orange and yellow shades	20 (50)	an exciting newer variety with clusters of double blooms
'Penelope Keith'	yellow	30 (75)	vigorous variety with good stems for cutting
'Pretty Polly'	light rose-pink	16 (40)	dense, rounded plant with medium-sized double blooms
'Queen Mother'	clear pink	20 (50)	semi-double blooms in clusters on a slightly spreading plant
'Starina'	scarlet and gold	12 (30)	novel bi-colour with a multitude of small, bright blooms
'Sweet Dream'	peachy apricot	32 (80)	upright grower with medium sized double blooms with a light scent
'Sweet Magic'	orange and gold	28 (70)	often described as the perfect patio rose, with neatly cupped blooms in clusters

'Angela Rippon'

'Pretty Polly'

'Sweet Magic'

Standards and weeping standards

Standard roses provide a mass of colour, add height to the garden and make particularly good specimen plants. A full standard has a stem around 36 in (90 cm) high; half standards are about 24 in (60 cm) high, and miniature standards only 16 in (40 cm) or so. All standards invariably consist of hybrid tea, floribunda, ground-cover or miniature roses grafted onto a suitably straight rootstock of the appropriate length.

Weeping standards are particularly spectacular. These are rambling and shrub roses grafted onto 56-inch (140-cm) rootstocks, with the long trailing shoots hanging downwards to give a gloriously tumbling cascade of flowers. Weeping they may be: sad they most definitely are not.

Standard roses can be planted in many different ways. They can be grown along one or both sides of a path in the front or back garden; they can be grown in containers on a patio, in cottage gardens, or in groups of three in a herbaceous border. Don't grow them on their own, as they will lose their full effect: they look much better side by side or in small groups. With container-grown roses it's now even possible to grow standards in pots on either a balcony or a patio.

Take care when selecting and planting standards. Some are extremely vigorous, producing upright, ugly heads. When this type of plant is used to give height to a rose bed, the colours should either contrast nicely and effectively with lower-growing plants or create an attractive blend.

Many repeat-flowering varieties can be grown as standards. Some of the most attractive are listed below.

Hybrid tea full standards (stem height 36 in/90 cm)

Variety	Colour	Remarks
'Fragrant Cloud'	geranium red	very fragrant
'Loving Memory'	crimson scarlet	classically formed blooms
'Margaret Thatcher'	light pink	fragrant
'Peace'	yellow edged with pink	very vigorous
'Silver Jubilee'	apricot and pink	a superb head of colour
'Super Star'	orange vermilion	fragrant
'Tequila Sunrise'	yellow and scarlet	a novel introduction

Hybrid tea half standards (stem height 24 in/60 cm)

'Alexander'	orange vermilion	good disease resistance
'Ingrid Bergmann'	dark red	fragrant
'Peace'	yellow edged with pink	very vigorous
'Silver Jubilee'	pink	fragrant, early
'Simba'	pure yellow	a ball of bright colour
'Sunblest'	yellow	very hardy
'Super Star'	orange vermilion	very fragrant

'Ballerina' grown as a shrub standard

Floribunda and ground-cover full standards (stem height 36 in/90 cm)

'Iceberg'	white	appears to be always in flower
'Korresia'	golden yellow	fragrant
'Lili Marlene'	deep crimson	flowers do not fade in sun or rain
'Suffolk'	blood-red	long flowering period
'Surrey'	pink	long flowering period

Floribunda, patio and ground-cover half standards (stem height 16–24 in/40–60 cm)

'Anna Livia'	clear pink	a useful pink with a good plant form
'Baby Masquerade'	yellow and orange	a pretty attraction
'Ballerina'	pink with a white eye	a striking colour mixture
'The Fairy'	light pink	small double flowers
'Intrigue'	dark crimson	darkest red in garden
'Kent'	white	the dark green foliage is a perfect foil
'Mandarin'	orange and gold	the perfect patio rose to grow on a standard
'Margaret Merril'	blush white	large blooms and a good plant structure
'Nozomi'	blush	a perfect umbrella
'Queen Mother'	soft pink	a beautiful ball
'Surrey'	pure pink	long flowering period
'Sweet Magic'	orange and gold	a striking colour with a good form
'Trumpeter'	bright scarlet	brilliant blooms and a good shape

Weeping standards (stem height 56 in/140 cm)

Albéric Barbier'	pale yellow	the only variety in this colour that is a true weeper
'Crimson Shower'	crimson scarlet	gives colour to the garden in midsummer
'Dorothy Perkins'	rose pink	a famous 'umbrella' rose
'François Juranville'	salmon pink	delicately formed blooms

All these varieties weep naturally, and don't require training. Like all standards, however, they must be well staked.

Old garden (heritage) roses

Many writers have tried to classify old roses according to age. But rose breeding has always been in a state of constant change, so this type of classification isn't very satisfactory.

For all the academic disagreement which has surrounded them, these roses are very beautiful. They include Bourbon, Hybrid Perpetual, Portland, Noisette and China

'Rosa Mundi'

'Charles de Mills'

hybrids, and the species roses *Rosa gallica, R. × damascena, R. centifolia, R. rugosa and R. × alba*, as well as all their many descendants. Some tea roses can also be described as old roses, including the silvery-pink 'La France', first sold in 1867, and the apricot-yellow 'Lady Hillingdon', dating from 1900. This category also includes some of the polyantha and pom-pom roses bred around the turn of the century.

Old roses have a great deal in their favour, including large numbers of delicately scented petals and a wide range of warm colours. Many of them, especially the summer-flowering ones, are surprisingly hardy and

disease-resistant. They can be planted together with repeat-flowering old roses, or even with modern shrub roses, to give a constant show of flowers from May until well into the autumn. Most old roses are more vigorous than modern floribundas and hybrid teas, and are sturdy shrubs with upright or arching shoots.

Some of the old-fashioned roses, such as Bourbon, Hybrid Perpetual and Moss roses, are fairly prone to disease. You can prevent this by hoeing in a compound fertiliser and mulching. If you provide the right conditions, these roses will go on blooming spectacularly for many years to come.

Old garden roses

Variety	Height in inches (cm)	Remarks
R. centifolia cristata ('Chapeau de Napoléon') (1827)	60–80 (150–200)	Centifolia rose, silvery-pink flowers, highly fragrant, summer-flowering
'Charles de Mills'	60 (150)	Gallica rose, fragrant double burgundy red flowers, summer-flowering
'Frau Karl Druschki' (1901)	40–48 (100–120)	Hybrid Perpetual rose, large, fully double pure white flowers with pink edges, repeat-flowering
'Gros Choux d'Hollande'	up to 80 (200)	Bourbon or Damask rose; large, double, highly fragrant rose-red flowers, summer-flowering

Old garden roses

Variety	Height in inches (cm)	Remarks
'Königin von Dänemark' (1816)	60–80 (150–200)	*R. alba* × *R. damascena* hybrid, full double silvery pink flowers with a dark centre; wild rose fragrance, summer-flowering, tolerates semi-shade
'Leda', also 'Painted Damask' (pre-1827)	40–60 (100–150)	Damask rose, globe-shaped, very fragrant milk-white flowers with crimson edges; sometimes repeat-flowering
'Maiden's Blush' (1797)	60–80 (150–200)	Alba rose (*R. alba*); sweet-smelling double white flowers; summer-flowering, tolerates semi-shade
'Mme Pierre Oger'	60 80 (150–200)	cream-reversed rose; a large, fragrant Bourbon which is good for cutting
'Mrs John Laing' (1887)	up to 80 (200)	Hybrid Perpetual rose, large fully double, fragrant silvery-pink flowers
'Rosa Mundi'	about 40 (100)	crimson and white striped flowers, a historic gallica that will grow in most gardens
'Souvenir de la Malmaison' (1843)	20–28 (50–70)	Bourbon rose, flat, fully double delicate pink flowers edged with white; fragrant; long flowering period.
'William Lobb'	about 60 (150)	very tall, with crimson to purple flowers; the most flamboyant of the moss roses

'Souvenir de la Malmaison'

'La Reine Victoria'

'William Lobb'

'Othello'

The results are a delight to all rose lovers. 'New English' roses include varieties that have inherited the scent and fully double flowers of old garden roses, and a number of enticing new colours have been added to the range. Like other varieties, these colours change constantly as the flower develops. In 'Charles Austin' for example, the flowers are an unusual apricot yellow colour with a tinge of scarlet. As the flower ages, it becomes almost white with a hint of delicate pink.

The flowers of 'New English' roses range from the single wild rose form through semi-double to fully double varieties. Most varieties have many petals, but the flowers also come in forms such as flat, open-cupped, globular and flat rosettes.

'New English' roses

It was the English rose grower David Austin who had the wonderful idea of crossing old roses with modern ones. He hoped to create roses with all the advantages of traditional Gallica, Damask and Centifolia roses (such as the fully double flowers and the wonderfully scented petals), combined with all the positive features of newer varieties (such as disease and rain resistance, and — most importantly — repeat flowering).

Repeat-flowering shrub roses

Variety	Colour	Height in inches (cm)	Remarks
'Abraham Darby'	apricot yellow flushed with pink	60–80 (150–200)	very fragrant
'Charles Austin'	apricot yellow	72–80 (180–200)	very fragrant
'Graham Thomas'	yellow	48–60 (120–150)	fragrant
'Heritage'	pink	40–80 (100–200)	small, cup-shaped fragrant flowers
'Othello'	dark scarlet	48–60 (120–150)	fragrant
'Swan'	yellowish turning to white	60 (150)	very large, fully double, delicately scented flowers
'Winchester Cathedral'	yellowish pink turning to white	48–60 (120–150)	large, double, fragrant flowers

Repeat-flowering varieties with double flowers (hybrid tea- and floribunda-like habit)

Variety	Colour	Height in inches (cm)	Remarks
'Cardinal Hume'	purple-red	28–36 (70–90)	medium-sized, globe-shaped, slightly fragrant flowers
'English Garden'	apricot yellow	28–36 (70–90)	large, rosette-shaped, slightly fragrant flowers; very free-flowering
'Warwick Castle'	deep pink	20–28 (50–70)	large fully double fragrant flowers

Repeat-flowering varieties with single to moderately full flowers

Variety	Colour	Height	Remarks
'Canterbury'	deep pink	28 (90)	highly fragrant, semi-double flowers
'Moonbeam'	white	48–60 (120–150)	moderately full
'Red Coat'	scarlet	60–72 (150–180)	large single flowers, slightly arching habit

Summer-flowering varieties with single to double flowers

Variety	Colour	Height	Remarks
'Constance Spry'	pink	60 (150)	very large, peony-like, sweet-smelling flowers
'Dr Jackson'	scarlet	60 (150)	large single flowers, very free-flowering, slightly arching habit

Summer-flowering varieties with single to double flowers

Repeat-flowering: 'Abraham Darby', 80–120 (200–300); 'Cressida', 72–120 (180–300); 'Hero', 72–100 (180–250); 'Leander', 100–120 (250–300)

Summer-flowering: 'Constance Spry', 100–140 (250–350); 'Shropshire Lass', 120–160 (300–400)

Apart from a few varieties which are not repeat-flowering, 'New English' roses are all repeat-flowering shrub roses. One of their best features is that most of them have rain-resistant petals, and they are also reasonably hardy.

'The Yeoman'
'Constance Spry'

Every rose smells different

Some roses have no fragrance. Some are scented, but keep it to themselves, and need to be appreciated from close quarters. Some other varieties, such as 'Fragrant Cloud', broadcast their fragrance far and wide — and every rose has a different fragrance. Though you might not think so, this is unusual in the plant world. Some roses are sweetly scented; others smell as fresh as the morning dew. Some rose fragrances have been compared to vanilla, vintage wine, raspberries or pineapple.

The strength of a rose's fragrance is also affected by outside factors: the better the growing conditions, the stronger the fragrance is likely to be. To bring out their fragrance, roses need to be grown in rich soil with plenty of compost, well-rotted manure or organic fertilisers, and require regular watering in long periods of drought. Warm, sunny weather also helps to bring out the full fragrance of roses.

It has also been shown that roses planted in heavy soils have a stronger scent than those in poorer, lighter soils. However, it's equally true that fragrant roses don't like soil that has been over-manured. And of course non-scented roses won't suddenly start giving off waves of scent, no matter how well you look after them.

Fragrance can be a very subjective thing: some rose catalogues and labels have a tendency to get carried away, and the actual flowers can prove a disappointment when you smell them.

'Westerland' growing with white delphiniums

'Evening Star'

'Fragrant Cloud'

'Fragrant Gold'

Scented roses

Hybrid teas

'Alec's Red'	cherry red
'Blessings'	salmon pink
'Blue Moon'	lilac
'Chrysler Imperial'	dark red
'Double Delight'	white-red
'Eroica'	dark red
'Evening Star'	white
'Fragrant Cloud'	orange
'Fragrant Gold'	deep yellow
'Keepsake'	old pink
'Papa Meilland'	dark red
'Paul Sherville'	peach and pink
'Rosemary Harkness'	orange-yellow
'Royal Albert Hall'	red and yellow
'Royal William'	deep crimson
'Selfridges'	lemon yellow
'Super Star'	orange vermilion
'Sutter's Gold'	golden yellow
'Troika'	bronze copper
'Whisky Mac'	bronze yellow
'Wimi'	pink edged with lilac

Shrub roses

'Lichtkönigin Lucia'	lemon yellow
'Radox Bouquet'	pink
'Westerland'	yellow and orange
'Conrad Ferdinand Meyer'	silvery pink
Rosa centifolia muscosa	pink

Climbers and ramblers

'Compassion'	salmon pink
'Lavinia'	pink
'Mme Alfred Carrière'	white
'The New Dawn'	pale pink
'Sympathie'	dark red
'White Cockade'	white

Floribundas

'Arthur Bell'	golden yellow
'Harvest Fayre'	apricot orange
'Korresia'	golden yellow
'Margaret Merril'	white
'Matangi'	orange red and white
'Shocking Blue'	lilac

Standards

'Fragrant Cloud'	orange
'Korresia'	golden yellow
'Margaret Merril'	white
'Silver Jubilee'	apricot-pink
'Super Star'	orange vermilion

31

Roses that may be suitable for cutting

Hybrid teas, with their beautifully formed buds and the elegant, lasting colour of their petals, are the most suitable roses for displaying in a vase. Some are also slightly fragrant, and some are very fragrant. Most classic hybrid teas have a single flower (which can be fully double) at the end of a more or less straight stem, so they make particularly good cut flowers.

Most of these are varieties which grow in the garden without too many problems, rather than commercially grown roses that have been forced in greenhouses exclusively for cutting.

Always cut roses in the early morning, when they're covered in dew; they'll have absorbed plenty of water from the soil, and this is when they'll be at their best. Put them in water as soon as possible. Don't cut too long a stem, as this will weaken the rose by depriving it of leaves. It may also be a good idea to leave roses alone for the first year after planting so they can build up their strength and produce an abundance of flowers in subsequent years.

However, hybrid teas aren't the only roses that look good in a vase. Modern shrub roses are ideal, and some of them flower in the garden before the first hybrid teas. One of the best

Red hybrid teas go particularly well with long-lasting white flowers such as carnations and Alstroemeria.

ROSES GROWN FOR SPECIAL PURPOSES

Hybrid teas particularly suitable for cutting

Variety	Colour	Remarks
'Alexander'	orange vermilion	long stems
'Congratulations'	deep pink	long stems
'Fragrant Cloud'	geranium red	very fragrant
'King's Ransom'	golden yellow	fragrant; long stems
'Loving Memory'	dark red	keeps its shape well
'Peace'	golden yellow edged with pink	disease-resistant
'Pink Pearl'	pearl	very long-lasting in water
'Selfridges'	bright yellow	long, strong stems
'Sunblest'	yellow	hardy
'Super Star'	orange vermilion	very fragrant
'Sutter's Gold'	golden yellow, shaded with pink	very fragrant
'Whisky Mac'	bronze yellow	distinctive colour

from this point of view is *Rosa hugonis*, the Golden Rose of China. Another yellow-flowered rose suitable for cutting is *R. pimpinellifolia* 'Maigold', which has semi-double flowers. And for a really good fragrance, try cutting *R. centifolia muscosa*, preferably with short stems so they don't wilt. There are plenty of other shrub roses which make good cut flowers, such as the highly fragrant 'La Reine Victoria' with its large pink flowers, and the rambling rose 'The New Dawn', with delicate pink, fully double flowers. There are even many floribundas, such as 'Anna Livia', which can be cut.

In hybrid teas, the side buds are pinched out to obtain longer, straighter stems; in floribundas and shrub roses, the opposite is true. The leading bud is removed as soon as a large number of side buds have come into flower. You should also remove all green buds where there is no sign of any colour appearing. This reduces evaporation, and makes the stems last longer when they are eventually cut.

Roses with attractive hips

The main classes of rose grown for their attractive, colourful hips are wild, shrub and some modern shrub roses. The hips stay on the roses a long time — often well into the winter — so they come in useful at a time when colour in the garden is in short supply. They can also look particularly good when they're covered in frost — and they attract birds, providing a major part of their diet in winter.

The rose hip is a false fruit, with the flesh providing a covering for the nut-like fruits themselves. While red is the most common colour for rose hips, other colours include yellow and brownish black, and there is even a rose with two-coloured hips: *R. sericea pteracantha* has red hips on a yellow stem.

Rose hips also vary greatly in size and shape. They may be round, pear-shaped or bottle-shaped. The earliest ripen in July (*R. sericea pteracantha*); others reach maturity in autumn. Roses with late-ripening hips include the dog roses (*R. canina*) and the eglantine or sweet briar, *R. rubiginosa* syn. *R. eglanteria*.

Some wild and shrub roses have a combination of beautiful flowers and attractive fruits, such as the Golden Rose of

R. moyesii *has bright scarlet hips.*

Roses worth growing for their hips

Name	Shape	Colour	Group
R. canina, dog rose	elongated	scarlet	wild rose
R. gallica 'Scarlet Fire'	round	cherry red, shiny, very attractive	shrub rose
R. glauca syn. *R. rubrifolia*	round or elongated, small	scarlet	wild rose
R. moyesii (and *R. moyesii* 'Geranium')	bottle-shaped with, long neck, hairy, very large	orange-red	wild rose
R. multiflora	small, round, grow in large numbers	red	wild rose
R. nitida	small, round	red	wild rose

China, *R. hugonis*, which flowers between May and June, and *R. gallica* 'Scarlet Fire', a bush growing to 6 ft 6 in (2 m) with large, scarlet flowers. Most semi-double and double varieties don't form hips.

R. rugosa

R. sweginzowii

Roses worth growing for their hips

Name	Shape	Colour	Group
R. pendulina, alpine rose	elongated, medium-sized	light red to orange	wild rose (thornless)
R. pimpinellifolia, Scotch rose	small, flat, round	brownish to deep violet	wild rose
R. pomifera, apple rose	large (up to 1–2 in/ 3 cm), round, thorny	bright red	wild rose; very popular with birds
R. rubiginosa syn. *R. eglanteria*, common sweetbriar	small, elongated	scarlet	wild rose, popular with birds
R. rugosa	flattened, round, very large and fleshy	red	wild rose; fruits and flowers appear together
R. sericea pteracantha	small, round	red with yellow stems	wild rose; very thorny
R. sweginzowii	elongated, bottle-shaped, long stem; large numbers	light red to orange-red	wild rose
R. virginiana	flat, round	shiny red; stays on stem for a long time	wild rose

'Frau Dagmar Hastrupp' has an abundance of hips

Planting for maximum effect

The first thing to consider before you even buy a rose is where you are planning to put it. Is the position suitable for roses, and will they flower freely and be reasonably free of disease? Generally speaking roses need a sunny position, though some will also tolerate semi-shade. They also need a certain amount of space around them; don't plant them near tall trees and shrubs, because they'll have to compete with the existing roots.

Apart from deciding which spot suits them best, you also have to decide which suits you best: where their colour and fragrance will give you as much enjoyment as possible. This means that scented roses should ideally be planted somewhere near the house, or near any place where you sit outside in fine weather. And if you want as clear a view of your roses as possible, particularly if they're standards, grow them either side of the garden path. Your miniature or ground-cover roses could be planted in the front garden, along the edge of a lawn, or in an island bed. The dark green of a well-tended lawn sets off pink, yellow and orange flowers to the very best advantage.

One possibility in a front garden is to grow a **rose arch** over the gate; you can continue the rose motif inside the garden by planting bedding or standard roses either side of the path or driveway. If yours is a typical, fairly small front garden, you should plant a single, relatively low-growing variety that won't take over the garden, but *will* flower for as long as possible each season. In a larger front garden with more than one rose

bed, plant one variety in each bed; otherwise the result will be an unattractive medley of colours. As a guide, if you have a front garden which measures 10 ft (3 m) from the gate to you front door, the ideal size of bed is 24 in (60 cm) wide, with two rows of roses.

If you find neatly mown grass or ground-covering shrubs such as cotoneasters boring in a front garden, why not try ground-covering roses instead?

Climbing and rambling roses will normally need some kind of discipline imposed on them if they are not to take ove

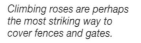

Climbing roses are perhaps the most striking way to cover fences and gates.

he whole garden. They can be grown in arches over a door, on a pyramid of wires or stakes, or on a fence, wall, trellis or arbour. Despite their size, they can be grown even in the smallest of gardens.

Shrub roses can provide a dramatic feature in gardens, whether they flower only once or repeatedly. This class of rose has been unjustly neglected in the past, but it includes many beautiful old roses, centifolia and moss roses, as well as 'New English' roses, which offer superb combinations of old and modern features. Plant these

A rambling rose ('Sanders White') can be seen here inching its way over a pergola.

either individually or in groups of three in any suitable position in the garden, or even in a vegetable bed or lawn. Shrub roses which are not repeat-flowering can be planted between other flowering shrubs to provide continuity of colour.

Wild roses can be used to make a hedge that will deter even the most determined burglar. Their flowers and hips will provide a splash of colour against what may be a rather monotonous hedge for the rest of the year.

Miniature roses can be grown in a rockery, and can also look good in the company of perennials. If you can avoid it, don't plant them singly; they look much more effective in groups of three or five of the same variety, though not more. And if you're very short of space, miniature roses also make good window box and container plants.

Rose arches, pyramids and trellises

Rose arches have undergone something of a revival recently, though true rose lovers have always sworn by them. They were an essential feature of many gardens in the past, but nowadays tend to be found only in large parks and rose gardens.

A climber or rambler grown over an arch, pergola or trellis can be a very good vertical substitute if you don't have the horizontal space for a rose bed. But it can also form a colourful and eye-catching showpiece for the garden, especially if grown on an arch over a gate or door. If you plant a number of arches 7–10 ft (2–3 m) apart, you have a magnificent pergola which will turn an otherwise unassuming path into a thing of beauty in its own right.

You can buy ready-made metal or plastic arches: the stems simply hook onto them, so there's no need to tie them in place. Buy one that's as wide as possible for the available space. This ensures that the shoots and flowers will get as much sun as possible, and makes it easier to provide protection in winter. It can also make spring pruning easier. The arches are available in various sizes; some are free-standing, and others can be attached to a wall. Some can even be fitted neatly together to form a pergola.

Roses growing over an arch

Pyramid-grown climbing rose

Plant one climbing rose either side of the arch; ideally you should choose a vigorous variety such as 'Sympathie' or Mme Alfred Carrière'. 'The New Dawn', which has very flexible stems, is an excellent rambler to grow over an arch.

Allow plenty of space either side of the rose: it needs an area of about 20 × 20 in (50 × 50 cm). Prepare the soil by digging it thoroughly, and make sure the rose is well watered and fed after planting.

Another way to display climbers and ramblers is to train them over a ready-made wire or plastic pyramid, or a home made one built of treated wooden posts. The ideal height for a pyramid is around 10 ft (3 m) with a diameter at ground level of 3–5 ft (1–1.5 m). Make sure it's firmly anchored in the soil to protect it from autumn gales, and include some cross-pieces to which the shoots can be tied.

Climbing roses can also be grown on an arch-shaped or rectangular trellis. This should be fitted so it's at least 6 in (15 cm) away from the wall. Roses grown on a hot south-facing wall will require extra feeding and plenty of water to get them established. Roses thrive better on pergolas because they allow air to circulate all around the plants and keep them healthier.

Climbing roses to grow over an arch

Variety	Colour	Remarks
'Climbing Cecile Brunner'	pink	beautiful miniature blooms on a big plant
'Coral Dawn'	coral pink	large, very fragrant hybrid-tea-like flowers
'Compassion'	salmon pink	very fragrant hybrid-tea-like flowers
'Paul's Scarlet Climber'	scarlet	large flowers, long flowering period, very free-flowering
'Summer Wine'	pink	vigorous modern climber with single flowers
'Sympathie'	dark red	hybrid-tea-like flowers, wild rose fragrance
'Wedding Day'	cream	a very vigorous rambler that is heavily scented

Making a rose hedge

A hedge made from wild roses will eventually become dense and impenetrable. It has the added advantage of attracting birds, as it provides a nesting place that's reasonably safe from cats and other predators, and its hips are a source of food in winter. It will also provide a dazzling display of colour, mostly in spring. A rose hedge is easy to look after and doesn't need drastic pruning: unlike other types of hedge, it can largely be left to its own devices.

Wild roses need plenty of room, so they should be planted in a row 6 ft (2 m) wide, with one or two plants per yard/metre. Besides providing a boundary for the outside edge of the garden, a rose hedge can also be used as a sight screen, or to provide shelter for other less about plants.

As the hedge grows it will need occasional pruning or thinning, but it should never be cut back drastically. Although wild roses are the most suitable type for hedges, you could also try the more vigorous floribundas such as 'Queen Elizabeth'. However these should be planted further inside the garden, as they aren't vigorous or dense enough to create privacy by screening it from passers-by. Alternatively you could use repeat-flowering shrub roses, which are suitable for a boundary hedge if your neighbours are amenable. Use upright-growing varieties which don't need staking such as 'Westerland' (see table opposite for further details).

Right *'Golden Wings'*

Far right R. sericea pteracantha

40

Wild roses suitable as hedges

Variety	Height in feet (m)	Flower colour, hips	Remarks
R. alba 'Great Maiden's Blush'	2.5-3 (0.8-1)	white flowers, very large hips	lime-hating; plant 2-3 plants per yard/metre when growing as a hedge
R. canina, dog rose	7-10 (2-3)	pale pink, almost white; light red, elongated hips	hips popular with birds; easy to grow; plant 40-80 in (100-200 cm) apart
R. gallica 'Scarlet Fire'	7-10 (2-3)	large scarlet flowers; very attractive cherry-red hips	vigorous, plant 10 ft (3 m) apart
R. 'Golden Wings'	48-68 (120-170)	clear, single yellow flowers	plant 3 ft (1 m) apart
R. multiflora	7-10 (2-3)	white; large numbers of small red hips	plant 60-80 in (150-200 cm) apart
R. 'Penelope'	40-60 (100-150)	double flowers, pale salmon pink	plant 30-40 in (75-100 cm) apart
R. pimpinellifolia 'Frühlingsgold'	8-10 (2.5-3)	very attractive yellow flowers	plant 7-10 ft (2-3 m) apart
R. rubiginosa, sweetbriar	7-8 (2-2.5)	pink flowers, elongated scarlet hips	hips eaten by birds. Plant 60-80 in (150-200 cm) apart
R. rugosa in variety	3-4 (1-1.2)	pale red flowers, very large red hips	lime-hating; plant 2-3 plants per yard/metre when growing as a hedge
R. sericea pteracantha	7-10 (2-3) or more	white, very free-flowering; red hips	very large (and attractive) thorns; plant 3 ft (1 m) apart
R. 'Westerland'	48-80 (120-200)	golden orange flowers	plant 3 ft (1 m) apart

Roses growing against a wall ('Parade')

Growing roses in the cottage-garden style

Cottage gardens are often so full of fruit and vegetables that the only space left for roses is on the fence.

Although the cottage garden is an increasingly rare phenomenon, roses are an essential feature of it. Sometimes you will still come across a cottage garden where old shrub roses provide a superb contrast to crops like cabbages and tomatoes. Lilac and honeysuckle were traditionally grown alongside roses, rivalling them in their fragrance. So were elder and blackthorn which, like roses, had the important advantage of fruits that could be made into jam or juice. Roses were also grown for medicinal purposes, and both rose hips and leaves were popular folk remedies. Rose water was believed to strengthen the heart; rose honey was a remedy for fevers; and rose hip tea was a cure for many different ailments.

Wild roses and other summer-flowering shrub roses also had an important practical use: they made an excellent hedge to keep livestock in and unwanted predators out. As this is rarely necessary today, we have grown to appreciate hedges made from roses like R. rugosa cultivars for their simple, natural beauty and often wonderful scent. These roses can give a garden that rustic look, without going to all the trouble of creating a cottage garden that's authentic down to the last detail. Most of these

roses are very vigorous, with good disease and pest resistance.

Old roses, modern shrub roses and rugosa roses such as 'Mrs John Laing', 'Conrad Ferdinand Meyer' and 'Marguerite Hilling' should ideally be planted as specimens in a flower or vegetable bed. Plant bush roses and small repeat-flowering

'Kiftsgate'	creamy-white, fragrant flowers	up to 33 ft (10 m) high
'Bobby James'	cream-coloured and fragrant	only 20 ft (6 m) high
'Seagull'	white flowers with golden filaments	13-16 ft (4-5 m) high
'American Pillar'	small, single deep-pink flowers with white centre	up to 20 ft (6 m) high
'Paul's Himalayan Musk Rambler'	small, fragrant violet-pink flowers	up to about 33 ft (10 m) high

shrub roses about a yard apart in groups of three for the best effect. Equally suitable for creating an old-fashioned look are the 'parents' of these roses: alba roses (*R. × alba*), damask roses (*R. damascena*), dog roses (*R. canina*), gallica roses (*R. gallica*), Scotch roses (*R. pimpinellifolia*), rugosa roses (*R. rugosa*) and sweet briar roses (*R. rubiginosa*).

Climbing and rambling roses can also be good for creating a cottage garden atmosphere, especially if they're grown over

a gate or door, or allowed to climb into a large tree with an open crown. Other trees suitable as a support for climbing roses include the yew (*Taxus baccata*) and the spruce.

Some rose varieties have passed the 'tree test' and are particularly recommended for this purpose. They are:

These and other vigorous climbers and ramblers are also ideally suited to growing over arbours. One particularly attractive variety is the 'New English' rose 'Constance Spry', a shrub rose 7-10 ft (2-3 m) high, which bears a profusion of double, myrtle-scented pink flowers in July.

Window boxes and other containers

The prime requirement for container-grown roses is enough space for their roots to expand. Roses have much bigger root systems than other plants (such as geraniums and fuchsias) that are commonly grown in containers. Miniature roses also need a lot of water, so they shouldn't share a container with other plants such as geraniums.

A container-grown standard rose can look good underplanted with vigorous, low-growing annuals such as sweet alyssum (*Lobularia maritima*) and creeping zinnia (*Sanvitalia procumbens*), which helps to break up the monotony of the container.

Roses grown in window boxes and other containers need plenty of good soil or, better still, a high quality potting compost. You should also keep them well watered, particularly for the first three weeks or so after transplanting while they're establishing their roots. From then on feed them regularly every two weeks until the end of July, using a specialist rose fertiliser.

Miniature roses such as the Meillandiana varieties can also be brought indoors for short periods, though they should be kept outside most of the time. This is because they won't flower a second time if they're brought indoors. Miniature roses should be pruned after they have flowered.

Far right *Miniature roses in an old terracotta container*

Below *Meillandiana varieties growing in a window box*

Container-grown roses

If you buy container-grown roses, they don't always have to be transplanted into open ground. One alternative is simply to place the pots inside a larger ceramic container, give them plenty of sun and water and feed them with a liquid fertiliser until early autumn. Many attractive hybrid tea and floribunda varieties in a wide range of colours are now sold in containers. These include full standards (40 in/100 cm) and — for smaller balconies and patios — half standards (24 in/60 cm) and miniature standards (16 in/ 40 cm), which are miniature and ground-cover roses.

Two groups of miniature roses are particularly suitable for window boxes, pots and bowls. Meillandiana roses are low-growing, and available in a rich variety of yellows, whites, pinks and reds, while Minijet roses are even more dwarfing, with smaller flowers to match.

Miniature roses can make an attractive temporary display. Plant them in a deep bowl so they can be removed after flowering and replanted elsewhere in the garden afterwards.

Miniature roses for pots, bowls and window boxes

Variety	Colour	Height in inches (cm)	Remarks
'Snowball'	white	4-12 (10-30)	slightly arching habit
'Baby Masquerade'	yellow/red	8-16 (20-40)	very bushy
'Mini Metro'	orange	12-20 (30-50)	very free-flowering
'Rugul'	yellow	8-16 (20-40)	slightly scented
'Little Artist'	red and white	8-12 (20-30)	very dwarf
'Longleat'	orange-red	8-16 (20-40)	bushy and compact

Companion planting with perennials

Roses can look particularly effective when they're grown in combination with other plants, especially with flowering perennials, or with grasses and other perennials grown for their foliage. All these plants will enhance the beauty of the roses (provided, of course, that the colours don't clash).

There's another big advantage in combining two types of plant: the perennials can provide colour when the roses aren't flowering, and distract the eye from the roses when they're at their least attractive. The cardinal rule is not to use too many different perennial species, and to make sure that the colours and shapes harmonise with one another. The tall blue spikes of delphinium flowers towering over an area of yellow bedding roses make one particularly striking combination. Another is a group of red hybrid teas or floribundas underplanted with the delicate tracery of white or pink gypsophila.

Floribundas, yellow achillea and blue perennial salvia

Matching growing requirements

Not all perennials make suitable companions for roses; some will obviously need different conditions. Most types of rose (apart from wild roses) will also need dead-heading, pruning and feeding, so it's important to leave some space around them for easy access. Carpeting perennials make particularly good edging for a bed of hybrid tea roses, especially as many of

them flower in spring, before the roses come into bloom. Examples might include *Iberis sempervirens* (which is, in fact, a sub-shrub), the clump-forming *Campanula carpatica* ('Blue' and 'White'), the various colours and varieties of *Aster dumosus*, gypsophila, *Cerastium bieber-steinii* and others.

All perennials grown as companions for roses need to be long-lived and sun-loving: this is no place for delicate species that need constant care and

attention. When you're laying out a new bed, plant the roses in groups and give the perennials room to expand. You may have to cut back or move ground-covering perennials if they start to smother the roots of the roses.

Perennials to grow with white roses

Try combining white floribundas, shrub and ground-cover roses with silver- or white-leaved perennials to achieve a pastel white effect. Examples of these include *Artemisia schmidtiana* 'Nana', *Achillea ageratifolia*, pearl everlasting (*Anaphalis triplinervis*), and *Cerastium biebersteinii*. Or to create a contrast with the roses, use blue-flowered *Linum perenne*, blue geraniums such as *Geranium grandiflorum* 'Johnson's Blue', *Erigeron* hybrids 'Adria' or 'Foersters Liebling', and the blue-violet *Veronica incana*. If you have enough space, grow catmint (*Nepeta × faassenii*). This clump-forming plant grows to a height of around 12 in (30 cm), tolerates dry conditions and goes particularly well with white hybrid teas.

Annual and perennial marguerites look particularly good with roses.

ight *Delphiniums and the yellow
ybrid tea 'Simba'*

elow *Roses, salvia and ornamental
rasses*

Perennials to grow with pink and red roses

Cool blue perennials can be used to tone down the warm pinks and reds of roses. Apart from Veronica incana, catmint and blue geraniums (which also do well with white roses), delphiniums are among the best companion plants for pink and red roses. They should be grown in small quantities to provide a splash of colour; otherwise they'll simply overwhelm the roses.

Lavender is a plant that has traditionally been used as an accompaniment to roses. Apart from its attractive flowers and its strong fragrance, it can also help to repel pests such as aphids and ants. Other blue-flowered plants suitable as companions for roses include latris, *Linum perenne* and scabious (*Scabiosa caucasica*). Bear in mind that very dark red roses don't make a very good match for blue-flowered perennials: use yellow or white varieties instead.

Yellow roses and blue perennials

Delphiniums, *Veronica longifolia* and all the other blue perennials mentioned above can also be grown with beds of yellow roses to very striking effect. Alternatively you can use tall, autumn-flowering Michaelmas daisies such as *Aster novae angliae* and *A. novii-belgii*, or their low-growing relative *A. dumosus*. Because they flower so late, Michaelmas daisies are an almost essential garden flower, and help to soften the blow of seeing your roses slowly fading as winter approaches. Blue and yellow is a particularly powerful combination of colours.

Above *Delphiniums are arguably the best of all plants to grow with roses (in this case 'Super Star').*

Left *Roses and alchemilla*

Grasses and wild roses

Wild roses and single-flowered shrub roses should be planted with perennials and grasses chosen to create a more natural, old-fashioned look. Examples include globe thistles (*Echinops pannaticus*), monkshood (*Aconitum*), and salvia (*Salvia nemorosa*). They also make good companions for many of the ornamental grasses such as blue oat grass (*Helictotrichon*), *Festuca scoparia* and *F. ovina*, which are also suitable as underplanting for floribunda and hybrid tea roses.

To create a really overgrown, natural feel to your garden, try combining wild roses and other shrub roses with perennial grasses such as the rather taller *Festuca mairii* (24–40 in/50–100 cm), *Molinia altissima* and *M. caerulea* (16–32 in/40–80 cm), *Panicum virgatum* 20–40 in/50–100 cm, with beautiful reddish-brown leaves that turn much darker in the autumn), and Chinese fountain grass (*Pennisetum compressum*, 32–36 in/80–90 cm). *Stipa barbata* (12–36 in/30–80 cm) is a very elegant ornamental grass, as is *Stipa capillata* (12–36 in/30–80 cm).

Moving older roses

You can't expect to take the whole of your garden with you when you move house, and you'll probably have to bid a fond farewell to much of it. In most cases it's less trouble simply to buy new plants when you arrive in your new home. But many people are particularly fond of their roses, and there's no reason why you shouldn't transplant them.

If at all possible, start preparing for the move in autumn by carefully digging up the roses. Cut off any damaged roots and then plant the rose at the same depth as before. Mix the soil around the plant with coarse compost, tread it down after planting the rose, and water it well. You should cut back all shrub and bush roses before starting to move them.

Roses grown in combination with blue oat grass (Helictotrichon)

Shrubs and conifers

Roses really do need to be grown in combination with other plants. As well as creating a look that's far more natural than a formal rose bed, companion planting helps to keep roses healthier.

For example, roses that are planted close to one another are much more likely to contract fungal diseases than those grown together with other plants.

Edging: Rose beds can be edged with low-growing shrubs such as box (*Buxus sempervirens*), which needs to be kept regularly pruned. Other shrubs can be left more or less to their own devices; for instance, the evergreen *Cotoneaster dammeri* var. *radicans* or 'Coral Beauty' will spill over attractively onto the path.

Another plant that's ideal for creating a boundary between a rose bed and a path is the rock rose *Helianthemum appeninum*, which reaches a height of only 6 in (15 cm) and flowers from June to September. The white flowering variety 'Wisley White' looks particularly good with pink roses.

Lavender, which like the evergreen *Iberis sempervirens* is actually a dwarf shrub, makes a beautiful frame for roses. Other good evergreen edging plants include the low-growing, mainly creeping *Euonymus* species *E. fortunei* var. *radicans* and *E. fortunei vegetus* 'Minimum'.

There are also a number of evergreen conifers that will do this job equally well. They include the creeping and prostrate species of juniper, *Juniperus communis* 'Hornibrookii', *J. communis* 'Repanda', *J. horizontalis* 'Glauca', *J. sabina* 'Tamariscifolia' and the spruce *Picea abies* 'Little Gem'.

Shrubs for interplanting with roses: These should be planned so that they bridge gaps in the year when the roses are not in flower, and set the roses off to best effect when they are. There are a number of attractive small shrubs which will do this without overpowering the roses. *Corylopsis pauciflora* has pale yellow flowers in March and April and reaches a height of 40 in (100 cm) or so. *Deutzia gracilis* bears white flowers in May–June, and grows to about

An old rambling rose dating back to 1827: 'Felicité Perpétue'

Roses surrounded by low box edges and pyramids

8 in (70 cm). *Caryopteris clandonensis* 'Heavenly Blue' has dark lilac flowers in August and September, and reaches a maximum height of about 40 in (100 cm). *Hypericum patulum* 'Hidcote Gold' has beautiful golden yellow flowers from July to October, and grows to between 4 ft and 5 ft (120 and 150 cm). Two shrubs with ornamental foliage that go well with roses are *Euonymus fortunei* 'Vegetus', which also has attractive berries in autumn, and cotton lavender (*Santolina chamaecyparissus*) which has evergreen aromatic foliage.

Any conifers grown with roses will probably need to be dwarf or slow-growing so they don't overrun their companions. Possibilities include the dwarf or Swiss mountain pine *Pinus mugo* var. *mughus*, which grows to only 32–40 in (80–100 cm); *Pinus pumilio* 'Glauca', 24–40 in (60–100 cm); the Hinoki cypress *Chamaecyparis obtusa* 'Nana Gracilis', only 16–20 in (40–50 cm); the yew *Taxus baccata* 'Repandens', 24–32 in (60–80 cm); and *Tsuga canadensis* 'Bennett', 36–72 in (100–200 cm).

When planting conifers, make sure you place them at least 4 ft (120 cm) away from the roses to allow for future growth. Note that the heights given above are 10–15 years after planting, not maximum heights.

With annuals

A certain amount of restraint is needed when combining annuals with roses. Annuals tend to come in fairly garish colours which can clash with the colours of the roses: this is particularly true of semperflorens and tuberous begonias, petunias and marigolds, which shouldn't be planted anywhere near roses. If you *do* use annuals, choose those which blend into the landscape and have a limited height and spread. Best of all are those with white and blue flowers, which can definitely enhance the appearance of roses, and the silvery leaves of cineraria, *Senecio bicolor*, which can greatly improve what might otherwise be a rather monotonous rose bed.

Annuals to grow with roses

Floss flower (*Ageratum houstonianum*): A popular hummock-forming bedding plant with mid- to deep-blue flowers, available in dwarf, medium and tall cultivars ranging in height from 5 to 24 in (12–60 cm). These plants can be difficult to propagate, and should therefore be bought.

Blue marguerite (*Felicia amelloides*): Grown for its attractive foliage and small blue aster-like flowers, this plant

The fragrant sweet alyssum (Lobularia maritima)

looks particularly striking with standard roses. Overwinter this plant in the same way as fuchsias. It can be propagated from cuttings, but this is difficult; it's easier to buy ready-grown plants.

Gypsophila: It's best to use the white varieties such as *Gypsophila repens* (6 in/15 cm), the large-flowered 'Maxima Alba' (18 in/45 cm) or *G. paniculata* 'Bristol Fairy' (30 in/75 cm). Sow gypsophila direct into the soil, and thin to 6 in (15 cm) apart.

Sweet alyssum (*Lobularia maritima*): A spreading plant reaching only 4 in (10 cm) in height, with large numbers of very small, fragrant white flowers in summer and early autumn. Use the white varieties such as 'Little Dorrit' rather than the purple-pink varieties such as 'Wonderland'. Sow where the plants are to flower; thinning isn't necessary.

Salvia: The annual varieties of salvia such as *Salvia farinacea* 'Victoria' (24 in/60 cm) and *S. hormium* 'Oxford Blue' (24 in/ 60 cm) create a wash of blue and violet in the rose bed which goes with roses of almost every colour and hue.

Creeping zinnia (*Sanvitalia procumbens*): Has yellow, daisy-like flowers and grows to a height of about 5 in (12 cm). Sow where the plants are to flower; full sun is essential.

Cincraria (*Senecio bicolor*): Highly recommended as a contrast plant for roses, with its distinctive silvery-grey leaves. Height 8-12 in (20-30 cm) depending on variety, with insignificant flowers. Best bought as a bedding plant.

Bulbs

Attractive though they are, bulbs should not be grown close to roses. This is because the foliage cannot be cut off after the plant has flowered, as the bulb needs it to regenerate. Tulips, hyacinths and even daffodils may be disturbed by the process of pruning and feeding the roses in spring. Even very small bulbs such as snowdrops, crocuses, scilla, eranthis and irises may be damaged by

rakes and hoes, no matter how careful you are.

The only roses that can have bulbs planted near them are shrub and wild roses, as these need relatively little pruning. Among the bulbs that can look good in this situation are species of ornamental garlic such as *Allium moly*, which bears bright yellow flowers in May and June.

The distinctive purple of annual Salvia farinacea 'Victoria'

When growing roses together with annuals and perennials, the main emphasis should be on bringing out the beauty of the roses in a natural-looking way. Hybrid teas and floribundas will need to be planted with different companions from those suitable for wild roses, whose natural beauty is enhanced by plants such as ornamental grasses and salvia.

Choosing what roses to buy

Before you pay out good money for a rose, make sure you're getting a premium-quality plant. It should have green shoots and smooth, well-ripened wood that doesn't yield to the touch when pressed. Roses sold in plastic bags should have a fresh, green look to them: if they've been stored too long, or in excessively dry conditions, they'll have a shrivelled look and may produce shoots prematurely. If you buy roses by mail order, you obviously can't check them before you buy, so use a reputable supplier.

A grade-one bare-root bush rose tree must have a minimum of two good shoots, each with the diameter of a thick pencil. The stems must look fresh, not shrivelled. The roots must be fibrous and in a moist condition, with a minimum length of 10 in (25 cm). Container-grown, containerised and prepack roses (see below) must meet the same standards as bare-root plants.

How roses are sold

Roses are sold in a number of different ways. Traditionally, growers lift them in autumn and sell them bare-rooted, either individually or in quantity (which makes them cheaper). Bare-rooted roses are often excellent value for money.

Plastic bags or boxes
Sometimes roses are sold bare-rooted in plastic bags or boxes. These are packed in moss or other organic materials, and are often sprayed with a harmless wax to prevent evaporation. The roots and shoots are trimmed to fit the bag or box, but still need pruning in the spring.

A rose planted with its own root ball

Containerised roses
A more reliable way of growing roses is to buy them containerised with their own root ball, ready for planting. These, too, are pruned ready for planting and are often covered with a thin layer of wax. Because the roots have their own root ball, they are likely to get off to a better start after planting.

Container-grown roses
Container-grown plants are even more likely to transplant well, as their roots will not be disturbed when they are moved. Before you buy a container-grown rose, check that it has actually been grown in the pot rather than containerised, and make sure it has a well-developed root system. If it doesn't have its own solid root ball, leave it in the pot when you plant it, and don't remove it from the pot until the autumn.

Choosing a supplier
There are obvious advantages in buying your roses from a local nursery or garden centre, especially one that you know has a good reputation. Apart from the convenience, you can easily check the quality and condition of the plants. Mail order is riskier, although you may have little choice if you want an unusual variety.

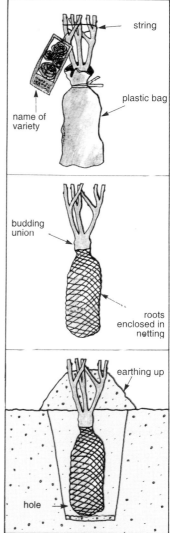

Planting prepack roses

Before you plant a prepack rose, cut off the string tying it together. Plants with the root ball tied up in netting should be left to soak in water for half an hour while you dig the hole. Remove the netting before you plant the rose, then fill the rest of the hole, and press the earth down firmly so the budding union is about 2 in (5 cm) below the surface. Then earth up the shoots with a mixture of soil and compost.

Planting bare-root roses

Cut away any diseased parts, and trim back thick roots. Put a mixture of compost and fertiliser into the bottom of the hole, and place the rose centrally, spreading its roots out. Push the soil back in to fill the hole, pressing it down well. Water the newly planted rose.

Right *Planting a container-grown rose*

Below *Bare-rooted and container-grown roses*

string

plastic bag

name of variety

budding union

roots enclosed in netting

earthing up

hole

Where to plant

Roses grow best in full sun, but not in positions which are too hot or too dry. If you grow roses against a south-facing wall, then they'll need extra irrigation. You should also bear in mind that even in winter the soil may dry out quickly in the sun, which is equally undesirable.

Plant roses in an open, well-ventilated position in a bed or border. Don't plant them too close to large trees and shrubs, as these will deprive the roots of water, and rain dripping onto the leaves will cause unsightly disease spot.

Generally speaking, roses should not be planted in north-facing or shady gardens, though there are many varieties which tolerate semi-shade and can manage on only a few hours' sun a day. Dark red varieties should always be planted in semi-shade, as this helps to prevent them from fading in the direct sunlight.

Soil

Don't plant roses where rhodo-dendrons and other lime-hating plants are growing, as roses dislike very acid soils. They'll grow well in slightly acid, neutral or slightly alkaline soils, with a pH of between about 6.4 and 7.5. If you're in any doubt, test the soil before planting (and at periodic intervals thereafter). Soil testing kits are inexpensive, widely available and easy to use, and show the lime, nitrogen, phosphorus and potassium deficiencies of the soil.

Roses are fairly tolerant of most soil conditions. Ideally, they should be grown in deep, well-drained humus-rich soil, so dig in some well-rotted manure or compost before planting roses. The one thing they do need is plenty of water, though they won't thrive in soil which is permanently damp.

Rose sickness

Sometimes, no matter how well you feed and water your roses, they may grow and flower badly even though there is no sign of any pests or fungal diseases. This is likely to be caused by rose sickness, which occurs when roses have been planted in the same place for more than about ten years. So when you plant new roses, either plant them where no roses have been grown before or, failing this, remove the top 20-24 in (50-60 cm) of soil and put it on the compost heap, then replace it with new soil from somewhere else in the garden. It was once believed that growing marigolds and other annuals prevented rose sickness, but recent trials have shown that this is not the case.

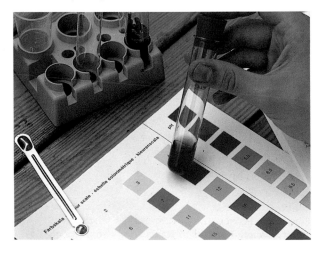

Simple do-it-yourself soil testing

Planting roses with certain other plants, such as lavender and marguerites, can help to keep the roses healthy.

Companion plants

Growing suitable companion plants between the roses in a bed can set off the display and provide an attractive background. Some plants will even give protection against pests. Low-growing ground-cover plants are best, though they make feeding difficult. Choose species with flowers and leaves whose colours will complement those of the roses. Pink roses, for example, look splendid against the grey-green leaves of herbs such as sage, as do red roses against silver-leaved plants. (See also pages 48–55).

The planting process

The best time to plant roses is in the autumn, because it allows them to develop strong roots before the winter frosts. These roots can then draw up water and nutrients from the soil in spring. Autumn planting helps to keep the wood ripe and prevent it from drying out.

Alternatively, provided that the frosts are over and roses are being sold in garden centres and elsewhere, you can plant in early March. At this stage the soil is likely to be damp from the winter rains, and again this will help the roses get off to a good start.

Before you plant roses, stand them in a bucket of water for 24 hours so the tissues can absorb as much water as possible. Make sure the budding union (the thickened area above the roots) also gets a good soaking. When you've planted the rose, water it again, very thoroughly; if the weather is dry when you plant it, water it every five days or so until the first strong shoots appear.

In northern areas, where the first frosts arrive early, it's better to leave rose planting until the spring. This is also a good idea if the soil is very wet in autumn, as this will prevent roots from forming.

All of the above applies only to bare-rooted roses: container-grown roses can be planted at any time of year. They can even be planted in midsummer, although in such cases they'll need generous watering.

Preparing the plant

Prune the roots back to a length of about 10-12 in (25-30 cm) before planting the rose: this will make it easier to fit into the hole, and will also encourage new roots to grow. Cut off any damaged roots.

Any shoots that grow from autumn-planted roses should be cut back in spring, as they'll probably have died back slightly in the frost. If the rose has particularly long shoots, cut these back by about a third of their length to make planting easier.

Roses planted in late autumn and spring should be pruned in the same way as older, established roses. Cut back long shoots of floribundas and hybrid teas by one third, and cut out any twiggy wood. Shrub and climbing roses should be cut back to leave only 3-5 stems. Prune the remaining shoots to a length of about 20 in (50 cm) to encourage new ones to form.

Preparing the soil

Many gardens suffer from compacted soil, especially if they are on heavy clay or a thin layer of soil with hardcore underneath. Plants won't thrive in these conditions because the soil is poorly drained; some areas retain moisture for a long time, so that in rainy periods the roots rot, and in dry weather they dry out. Proper preparation of the soil is essential if your roses are to grow well and produce plenty of flowers. For roses the soil should be worked over with particular care, because the roots will form a dense layer between 4-20 in (10-50 cm) below the surface. Some roses grafted onto *R. canina* rootstocks may grow considerably deeper than this. Ideally, the soil should be dug over and loosened several weeks before planting to give it time to settle.

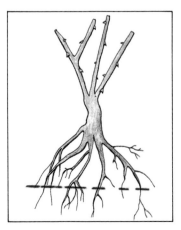

Prune the roots slightly before planting.

PLANTING ROSES

Support

Bush roses don't need support, while hedging roses support each other. Ramblers are supported on trellises, and for standards and climbing roses proper support is also vital.

Standards are tied — loosely at first — to a stake inserted firmly near the centre of the planting hole, on the windward side. Climbers grow along wires fixed horizontally to a fence or wall.

Roses will thrive in a well-drained soil and a sunny position — in front of a wall or a fence, for example.

Planting and watering

Proper preparation of the soil will make a significant difference to the vigorousness and successful flowering of a rose. You should dig over the soil to an average depth of about 12 in (30 cm), and ideally, except in the case of light, sandy soils, you should also break up the layer beneath this with a fork.

Dig a planting hole broad and deep enough for the roots to spread, and for the bud union to be buried about 2 in (5 cm) deep. Fill the hole loosely with a mixture of garden soil and compost, and then press it down firmly so there's a slight hollow round the plant. Finally fill this hollow gradually with water till it starts to spill over the top. Do this several times after planting. Generally speaking you only need to water in newly planted bushes when you're planting in the spring.

When you're planting standard-grown roses, hammer the stake firmly into the soil first and then plant the rose about 2-3 in (5-8) cm away from it. Protect the stem against damage with a piece of tyre rubber, and make sure the stem isn't tied to the stake too tightly.

When you're planting climbing roses, the hole should be around 4-8 in (10-20 cm) away from the wall. Plant the bud union 2-4 in (5-10 cm) below the surface, and arrange the roots so that they face away from the wall.

Above *Give roses a good soaking before you plant them.*

Left to right:

Make a small heap of earth in the hole and spread the roots over it.

Place the bud union about a hand's breadth below the surface.

Press the earth down firmly.

Water very generously.

Earth up with soil and compost.

Planting distances

How far apart you plant your roses will depend on the height and spread of the individual varieties, as well as the soil type and the local climate.

The following distances are recommended for both **floribundas and hybrid teas** planted in a rose bed. Taller varieties should be planted 30 in (75 cm) apart, or three plants per square yard/metre; medium-sized roses 24 in (60 cm) apart, or four plants per square yard/metre, and smaller ones 20 in (50 cm) apart, or five plants per square yard/metre.

Repeat-flowering shrub roses are most effective if they are grown individually as specimen shrubs, but they can also be grown in small groups of three to five. In the latter case, plant the roses 40-48 in (100-120 cm) apart for taller, more spreading varieties, and 32-40 in (80-100 cm) for more compact ones. When planting rose hedges or rows of shrub roses, plant larger varieties 32-40 in (80-100 cm) apart and smaller ones 28-32 in (70-80 cm) apart.

Summer-flowering shrub roses should normally be grown singly, but if you do grow more than one together, use a planting distance of 60-80 in (150-200 cm) — or 40 in (100 cm) if you're planting a hedge.

The majority of vigorous **climbing and rambling roses** should be planted about 8-10 ft (2.5-3 m) apart, although some of the slower-growing ones can look well if they're planted about 7 ft (2 m) apart.

With **ground-cover roses,** planting distances vary greatly depending on the growth habit of the different varieties and species, so follow the grower's instructions.

As for **miniature roses,** plant tall varieties 14 in (35 cm) apart, or eight per square yard/ metre; medium-sized roses nine to the square yard/metre, and small ones eleven to the square yard/metre. Miniature roses that are grown in window boxes need only be planted 8-10 in (20-25 cm) apart.

Where **standard roses** are grown in rows or groups, they should be planted with at least 7 ft (2 m) between each one, and weeping standards somewhat further apart. Half standards and miniature standards can be grown 40 in (100 cm) apart — but they lose their character if they're planted too close together, looking rather like a line of soldiers.

Looking after your roses

Dead-heading

Once the flowers of a rose have faded, a rose hip forms. On summer-flowering and wild roses the hips are usually allowed to grow: they're decorative, and they also provide food for birds in autumn and winter. As a rule, then, these roses aren't usually dead-headed.

On the other hand hybrid teas, floribundas, repeat-flowering shrub and climbing roses should all be dead-headed regularly so that the plant devotes its energies to forming new flowers rather than seeds. Snip off the flower head and the two fully-grown leaves immediately below it, removing only about $\frac{1}{4}$ inch (5 mm) of the stem. Don't cut off any more than this; the more you cut off, the longer it will take for new flowers to grow (though the quality of the new blooms will be better).

In the case of floribundas, cut off the flower head immediately above the top set of leaves. If you remove any more than this you'll delay the appearance of the next flower by several days. There are a couple of exceptions to this rule: if the stems are very long and spindly, cut them back more severely, removing three or four buds so that the plant develops into a strong, well-formed bush. And if you are cutting roses for display, you can cut them with longer stems.

Suckers are shoots which grow from the rootstock. As a rule they're fairly easy to recognise, as they tend to have smaller, paler-coloured leaves. Remove them by loosening the surrounding soil and then twisting the sucker off, or sever it at the base with a pair of secateurs. Don't leave a stump, as this is likely to grow into a new sucker.

Watering, hoeing and mulching

Roses that grow or flower badly, or are vulnerable to disease, may not be getting enough water. Roses need a really good soaking in hot, dry weather: they should be given about 4 gallons per square yard of soil (20 l/m²), so that the water sinks at least 12–20 in (30–50 cm) into the ground. Water in the early morning or late evening, and place the hose right up close to the plant with the tap turned only half on. Don't spray the leaves themselves, as this makes them more prone to fungal diseases — and keep sprinklers well away from roses.

Roses need plenty of air, so if the soil has hardened after heavy rain followed by sunshine

A straw mulch: alternative materials include dead leaves or bark.

Looking after roses in summer

Dead-head regularly, except in the case of wild roses. Remove suckers. Tie in the stems of climbers and ramblers. Water well in dry weather. Provide a mulch, feed regularly, hoe to keep the soil loose and take steps to prevent pests. Dead-head standard roses in the same way as hybrid teas: remove the flower head itself and the top two leaves, leaving an outward-facing bud.

Above *Snip off dead flower heads immediately, and use them as compost.*

Right *Neatly dead-headed roses ('Alexandra')*

is worth hoeing it very gently. This will break up the soil without damaging the roots. If you mulch the soil, it will remain well-drained, damp and weed-free: place a layer of organic material such as compost, dried grass clippings, leaves, straw or well-rotted manure around the base of the plant in spring. By the autumn the mulch will have rotted down, and can then be used to earth up the plant the following winter.

Feeding roses properly

Like other flowering shrubs, roses need something more than a diet of water and tender loving care to survive. They must also supplied with the right balance of nutrients, particularly nitrogen (N) for leaf development, phosphorus (P) for flower formation and potassium (K) to create strong, ripe shoots. Roses also need a good supply of trace elements; the most important are iron and magnesium.

Older, established roses should be fed twice a year. Newly planted ones need to form hair roots before they are fed, so give autumn-planted roses their first feed in April or May of the following year, and don't feed roses planted in the spring until the end of June. If you don't feed your roses they will be more susceptible to pests and diseases, because the processes of growth, bud and flower formation will all slow down.

Roses grow best in free-draining, humus-rich soil which has had regular additions of compost or well-rotted, strawy manure; most garden centres sell bags of horse manure and dried or composted cow manure. If you buy fresh manure, put it onto the compost heap and leave it to rot until it is brown and crumbly, with an earthy

smell. Place a 2–4-inch (5–10-cm) layer round your roses in early spring.

You should also add an organic fertiliser such as bonemeal or pelleted cow manure, as the nutrients in these fertilisers often take months to take effect. Work in an organic mineral fertiliser such as Growmore, or a special rose fertiliser with trace elements (e.g. Toprose). Do this as early as possible in spring (i.e. in late February or early March), using about 2 oz per square yard (60 g/m^2).

The next time to feed roses is around the middle of June, using the same quantities as for the spring feed. This will encourage the second flush of

flowers in repeat-flowering roses, and build up the strength of summer-flowering ones.

Finally, between October and December, feed your roses again with potassium sulphate. This will help to ripen the wood, and make the roses much hardier in winter. Again, use 2 oz per square yard (60 g/m^2).

Roses need humus-rich soil.

'Selfridges', a hybrid tea, is good for cuttings.

If possible, add the feed to the soil during wet weather. If you have to use it in dry weather, water it in well afterwards. Never sprinkle fertilisers onto leaves and flowers as this will cause scorch. And never overfeed roses: the rule of thumb is to hoe in a handful of organic mineral fertiliser once in spring and once after the first flush of flowers.

Well-rotted farmyard compost is ideal for roses.

Foliar feeding

Foliar feeding (spraying a dilute liquid fertiliser directly onto the leaves) has become popular for houseplants, and is sometimes used for roses too. It is not really necessary unless the roses cannot take up enough nutrients through the roots — in a prolonged dry spell, for example. However, it can produce some blooms of dramatic size for special displays.

It's easy to make your own liquid fertiliser by steeping two buckets of sheep manure in a large barrel of water. Apply one large bucket to each square yard/metre.

Pruning

Roses, particularly hybrid teas and floribundas, need to be pruned every year. If left un-pruned, they will grow tall and straggly; suckers will form, the stems will die back, the leaves will fall off and both flowering and growth will be poor. The only exceptions to this rule are wild roses and other summer-flowering shrub roses, which need very little pruning except when they grow too large and require thinning.

When to prune

Prune roses in spring, as soon as the last hard frosts are over. In practice this will be from mid-March to early April, or earlier in milder areas. In fact the roses themselves will tell you when they need pruning: when the leaf and flower buds begin to swell and start changing colour, it's time to reach for your seca-teurs. This will also indicate which shoots have survived the winter. If you prune roses in autumn, you may have to prune them again later: autumn prun-ing is very risky, and will delay the start of flowering the follow-ing year.

Ground rules

Not all roses should be pruned back hard every year: different classes of rose need different amounts of pruning.

Make sure the cut is in the right direction, and at the right distance from the bud. If you cut at too sharp an angle, or too close to the bud, it will wither.

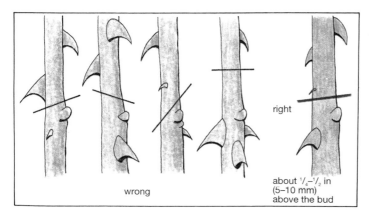

right

wrong

about $\frac{1}{4}$–$\frac{1}{2}$ in (5–10 mm) above the bud

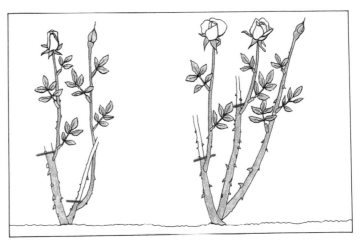

Roses should be pruned back to just above a bud — but first cut out any old, diseased or frost-damaged wood and any crossed or overcrowded stems. Make a diagonal cut above an outward-facing bud. Don't cut too close to the bud or it will wither, and the shoot that forms from it will be more prone to damage. The cut should be about $\frac{1}{4}$-$\frac{1}{2}$ inch (5-10 mm) above the bud: any further, and dieback will occur.

The more severely you cut back a stem, the longer and more vigorous the new shoots will be. Prune low-growing roses hard, and vigorous ones more gently. Make sure your secateurs are sharp so they make a clean cut; good modern secateurs will normally have removable blades.

Standard roses should be pruned in the same way as hybrid teas.

Above *The harder you prune, the more vigorous the new shoots will tend to be.*

Below *It's important to prune in the right place.*

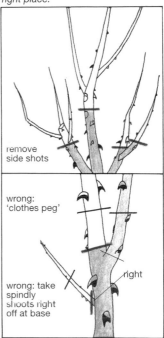

remove side shots

wrong: 'clothes peg'

wrong: take spindly shoots right off at base

right

Pruning different types of rose

The hybrid teas and floribundas

Prune taller hybrid teas back to 4-6 buds, or a height of about 24 in (60 cm). Lower-growing varieties should be pruned back to leave 3-4 buds, or a height of 12 in (30 cm). When counting buds, always start at the bottom (the bud union), but don't

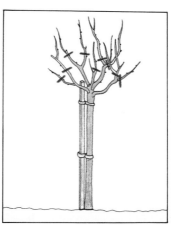

A standard before and after pruning

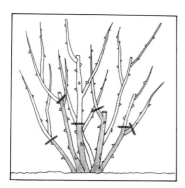

Floribunda before and after pruning

spend hours laboriously counting buds. The main thing is to prune just above a bud every time.

Normally, the shoots will need to be cut back by about two thirds of their total length. If you want to grow roses for cutting, prune them back by one or two extra buds to give longer stems.

As floribundas are usually grown in groups, and grow at about the same rate, prune

them all back to the same height. The individual shoots of hybrid teas grow at very different rates, so the best rule is to prune long shoots lightly to leave about seven buds, and cut weaker shoots down to two or three buds. If the shoots are very weak and spindly, cut them right back to 0.1 in (2-3 mm) above the bud union.

Shrub roses

Species and summer-flowering shrub roses should be left alone as much as possible, as they flower on old wood. Dead, diseased or overcrowded stems should be pruned right back to ground level. Older roses planted more than about five years ago can benefit from severe pruning to rejuvenate the rose. Cut back whole stems to ground level, using a saw if necessary.

These pruning rules also apply to repeat-flowering shrub roses: since these mostly flower on the side shoots, you should restrict pruning to occasional thinning. To encourage new growth, cut back short shoots to 3-5 buds, and longer ones by about a third of their length.

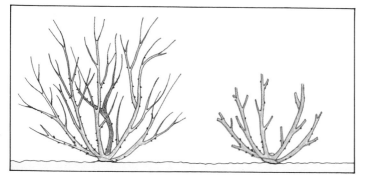

Pruning repeat-flowering shrub roses: remove old stems (shown in red). If the rose has been damaged by frost, cut the main stem back less severely and the side stems more severely.

Pruning climbing roses: train the larger, stronger stems into a fan, and then prune moderately.

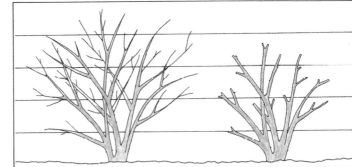

Climbing and rambling roses

Rambling roses need as little pruning as possible, and the young sucker-like shoots should be left well alone. The best flower clusters will grow on these vertical shoots, which develop from the previous year's horizontally trained shoots. Cut back the 'new' shoots to between two and five buds, and remove any old or frost-damaged wood which is unlikely to flower well. Prune right down to the ground to encourage new growth.

Climbing roses can also be pruned back very severely if they're no longer growing or flowering satisfactorily, and if they're not producing enough new shoots. Prune summer-flowering roses immediately after they have flowered, and repeat-flowering ones at the same time as most other roses, in March or April.

Standard roses

Whether you're looking at full, half or miniature standards, the rule for pruning is the same as for hybrid teas: reduce by two thirds. Sometimes you may have to prune the rose back harder (if, for instance, the crown is developing too vigorously, or the stems have been damaged by frost). Again, you should prune back to an outward-facing bud to build up a well-balanced structure.

Weeping standards should be pruned in the same way as ramblers (which is, after all, exactly what they are). As well as cutting out old wood, remove some of the new shoots if there are too many of them. Shorten stems which are touching the ground. Most weeping standards flower only once, and should therefore be pruned after flowering.

Miniature roses

Prune these in the same way as floribundas and hybrid teas. If you're using the roses as edging, they can simply be cut back with a pair of shears to about half their height.

Remove suckers right back to the base if possible, or down to ground level if not.

What causes poor growth?

Roses are very tolerant plants, but walk down any suburban street and you will see roses that have been badly neglected. As a result they are spindly and unattractive, producing few if any flowers. Neglected roses are also more susceptible to pests and diseases, especially when they're also being grown in the wrong place.

Leaf damage

Frost damage causes crinkled leaves with brown edges. Simply prune the affected stem back to the next pair of undamaged leaves. Large yellow areas spreading outwards from the leaf stalk and veins may be caused by one of three things: waterlogging, pollution or careless use of weedkillers. If the cause is waterlogged soil, dig up the rose, provide proper drainage in the bottom of the hole, cut off spindly roots, prune the crown and replant the rose. Otherwise, be very sparing in cutting the stems back, as the plant needs as many leaves as possible.

Under-watering causes yellow blotching on the leaves and premature leaf fall. This problem should be dealt with by watering very thoroughly at a rate of about 4–6 gallons per square yard (20–30 l/m^2).

Too much sun can make dark red varieties turn black and scorched. This is only likely to happen if the roses are grown on a south-facing wall or near a paved patio. The only cure for this problem is to move the rose somewhere else.

Nutrient deficiencies

Nitrogen deficiency results in the young leaves remaining small and pale green, sometimes

Roses badly damaged by rain

A very obvious case of iron deficiency

with red spots on their upper surfaces. The leaves may also fall off. Feed the rose with a high-nitrogen fertiliser.

Phosphorus deficiency is less common. It causes violet-brown stripes on the edges of the leaves, short, weak stems and leaf drop. You can deal with it by applying a handful or so of bone meal over each square yard/metre, preferably in the early spring.

Potassium deficiency is indicated by brown edges to the leaves and pale-coloured flowers. Give the rose an extra large dose of sulphate of potash fertiliser in early spring.

Magnesium deficiency causes a yellowish-red colouring to the leaves and premature leaf fall. Use a compound fertiliser containing magnesium, or hoe in 1 oz per square yard (30 g/m²) of magnesium sulphate and then water thoroughly.

Manganese deficiency produces yellow edges between the veins of older leaves. This may be a particular problem with roses grown in very acid or alkaline soils. Use a fertiliser containing manganese.

Iron deficiency: if there is too much lime in the soil, it may cause chlorosis: the leaves turn yellow, and only the veins remain green. Use a fertiliser

which acidifies the soil, such as ammonium sulphate or potassium sulphate. For a more rapid effect, use Murphy Sequestrene.

Bud damage

If the buds are withered and fail to open, they've probably been damaged by thrips. Cut off the affected shoots and throw them away (don't use them as compost), or spray with an insecticide such as Hexyl. This problem can also be caused by too much shade, or by waterlogging. Bud rot is caused by the botrytis fungus, which also affects the leaves and flower stalks. Here again, the only solution is to remove and dispose of the affected parts.

The leaves and young shoots of roses may also be damaged if they are planted too close to a fence or trellis treated with a preservative such as creosote, which is harmful to plants. This can be a particular problem in hot weather, when the preservative gives off fumes. To avoid this problem, use non-toxic preservatives or pressure-treated wood. The only cure is to remove the affected shoots — but take off as little as possible, so that the leaf and flower buds are left.

Roses that are generally resistant to disease

Apart from colour and fragrance, one of the main aims of rose growers is to develop new roses that are more resistant to fungal diseases. Most shrub and climbing roses now have good disease resistance, but some hybrid teas and floribundas are still very susceptible to leaf diseases. Of course, none of these roses is totally resistant to fungal or viral diseases, but they are fairly likely to be resistant if they're grown in a suitable position and properly fed.

The term 'semi-shade' in the table below indicates that this variety can manage on only a few hours' sunshine a day, though its colour will be stronger if it's grown in full sun.

'Blessings'

'Fragrant Cloud'

Hybrid teas and floribundas with good disease resistance

Variety	Colour	Height in inches (cm)	Remarks
'Alexander'	orange vermilion	40–60 (100–150)	good for cutting
'Blessings'	coral pink	40 (100)	good for cutting
'Colour Wonder'	salmon pink	32–40 (80–100)	very fragrant
'Dawn Chorus'	deep peach	32–40 (80–100)	an exciting new variety
'Elina'	pale creamy yellow	40–48 (100–120)	fragrant
'Evening Star'	pure white	40–48 (100–120)	fragrant
'Fragrant Cloud'	geranium red	32 (80)	very fragrant
'Ingrid Bergmann'	dark red	32–48 (80–120)	very free-flowering
'Keepsake'	pink	40–60 (100–150)	perfect form
'National Trust'	crimson scarlet	32–40 (80–100)	a neat and tidy bush
'Peace'	yellow edged with pink	40–80 (100–200)	very vigorous
'Precious Platinum'	dark red	40–48 (100–120)	good colour
'Royal William'	crimson velvet	40–80 (100–200)	the healthiest dark-red scented hybrid tea ever
'Selfridges'	bright yellow	40–80 (100–200)	good for cutting
'Silver Jubilee'	salmon pink	28–40 (70–100)	free-flowering
'Sutter's Gold'	golden yellow	28–36 (70–90)	fragrant

Floribunda roses

Variety	Colour	Height in inches (cm)	Remarks
'Amber Queen'	amber yellow	24–40 (60–100)	fragrant
'Anna Livia'	pink	36–40 (90–100)	good for cutting
'Anisley Dickson'	salmon pink	32–40 (80–100)	good for cutting
'Betty Prior'	salmon pink	32–40 (80–100)	robust
'Bucks Fizz'	soft orange	40–48 (100–120)	strong, upright growth
'Chorus'	crimson	20–28 (50–70)	semi-shade
'Escapade'	magenta pink	32–40 (80–100)	fragrant
'The Fairy'	pink	24–40 (60–100)	spreading habit
'Intrigue'	very dark red	32–40 (80–100)	surprisingly healthy for this colour
'Korona'	orange-red	32–40 (80–100)	bright colour
'Korresia'	golden yellow	32–40 (80–100)	fragrant
'La Sevillana'	orange-red	36–48 (90–120)	glossy foliage
'Märchenland'	bright pink	40–60 (100–150)	fragrant
'Margaret Merril'	pearl white	32–48 (80–120)	very fragrant
'Melody Maker'	light vermilion	40–48 (100–120)	bright and very free-flowering
'Mountbatten'	mimosa yellow	40–80 (100–200)	very vigorous
'The Queen Elizabeth Rose'	pink	40–48 (100–120)	good for cutting, very tall
'Rob Roy'	dark red	36–44 (90–110)	good for cutting
'Royal Occasion'	orange	32–44 (80–110)	fragrant
'Southampton'	soft apricot	40–60 (100–150)	tall and luminous
'Tango'	orange and yellow	40–80 (100–200)	will make a good shrub
'The Times Rose'	crimson-scarlet	32–60 (80–150)	the healthiest floribunda
'Trumpeter'	vermilion orange	20–32 (50–80)	a good short bedding rose

'Remember Me'

'Amber Queen'

'City of Birmingham'

Common diseases and pests

If roses are attacked by pests, it may be because they're not being properly looked after. Heavy, prolonged rain can also cause fungal diseases and make roses more vulnerable to pests. You may be doing all that you can — planting your roses in the best positions, choosing disease-resistant varieties, and watering and feeding them properly — but if they're still suffering from pests or diseases you need to take positive action.

Fungal diseases

Mildew
The stems, buds and leaves are covered in a white coating. Mildew can be prevented by buying mildew-resistant varieties, avoiding over-feeding, watering well in dry weather and spraying the roses and the surrounding soil with horsetail infusion (see page 79) in spring and autumn. Cut off affected shoots and spray two or three times at three-week intervals from June with Benlate, Roseclear or Multirose.

Black spot
Leaves are covered in round black or brown spots and fall prematurely. Collect and dis-

Black spot

pose of all infected leaves (*don't* put them on the compost heap), feed regularly and mulch to improve humidity at the roots. Direct methods of prevention include sprinkling wood ash round the plant and spraying it with nettle infusion (see page

Mildew

79) or, in serious cases, spraying with Benlate, Roseclear or Multirose.

Rust
Yellow swellings on the undersides of the leaves, turning black in autumn; also causes premature leaf fall. Can be prevented by mulching well, choosing rust-resistant varieties and regularly picking up fallen leaves. Spray with horsetail infusion (see page 79) and repeat if necessary, or spray with Systhane.

Pests

Aphids
These green, black or reddish insects damage the leaves, buds and young shoots of roses and leave a sticky secretion on the

Rust

leaves. Lavender, nasturtiums and cress are believed to repel aphids when planted underneath roses, and the aphids can be dislodged simply by spraying them with a powerful jet of water. If necessary, spray your plants with Murphy's Systemic Insecticide.

Common spider mites
Small white spots and webs on the undersides of the leaves. Can be prevented by mulching, and by spraying with horsetail or nettle infusions (see page 79) or spraying with Malathion.

Rose slugworm
The green larvae eat the leaf tissue but not the veins, producing a skeleton effect. Spray with tansy solution (see page 79; this can also be used against rust and mildew), or in serious cases spray with Sybol.

Leafhoppers
Pale yellow jumping insects which suck the sap from the undersides of the leaves, creating white blotches. Eggs are laid on young shoots. Prevent by spraying with tar oil wash in winter to get rid of the eggs, or treat in spring and summer by spraying with Sybol.

Red spider mite
Small red mites which live in large numbers on the undersides of the leaves. Leaves wither and fall off. Prevent by mulching and watering well in dry weather, and spraying with nettle, horsetail or soap and

Above *Aphids*

Left *Leathoppers*

alcohol solution, or control by spraying with Malathion.

Leaf-rolling sawfly
Leaves are rolled up into a cone shape. Cut off and throw away the affected leaves, or spray with Sybol.

Ants on a rose may indicate the presence of aphids. The ants are harmless, but they do not eat the aphids; instead they 'milk' them. Use a spray such as Pyrethrum, which will kill the aphids but leave the ants unharmed.

77

Environmentally friendly ways of preventing pests and diseases

As people become increasingly aware of environmental issues, they are turning away from highly toxic pesticides and weedkillers. Long before these chemicals were developed, people used natural materials obtained from garden plants for this purpose, and these are now starting to become popular again. It is easy to make infusions from plants such as nettles, horsetail, comfrey and wormwood: if you don't have access to these plants, you can buy them in dried form from herbalists, and even from some garden centres.

A word of warning: like some commercial preparations, some plant infusions contain dangerous or even poisonous substances — and they don't have

instructions on the packet! So always take suitable precautions to keep them away from eyes, mouth, lungs and skin.

Liquid manures
Liquid manures are mainly used to promote growth; they are applied to the soil rather than being sprayed directly onto the plant. Liquid manures can be used both to create stronger plants and as a preventive spray against aphids and spider mites. A liquid manure can be made by soaking dry sheep droppings in rainwater for about four days.

Herbal infusions
Soak the leaves and stems in water for 24 hours, then simmer the plants in the same water over a low heat for about half an hour. Allow to cool, and strain.

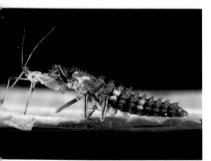
Ladybird larvae are also natural predators on aphids.

Alternatively, you can pour hot water over the fresh or dried plants, leave to stand for 10-15 minutes and then strain.

Recipes

Nettle infusion

Mix 5 oz (150 g) of powdered nettles with 2 gallons (10 l) of water in a plastic container, and leave the mixture to ferment for seven to ten days. Then dilute with ten parts of water. Pour round the roots of roses, or

dilute well and pour onto the leaves. Use this infusion after about four days, diluted one part to 50 parts of water, against aphids and spider mites.

Horsetail infusion

Dilute 3 fluid ounces (8 ml) of horsetail extract with 1 gallon (5 l) of water. To control black spot spray roses (including the young shoots) regularly, preferably in dry, sunny weather. The infusion works though the leaves and roots.

This infusion can also be made by soaking 2 lb (1 kg) of fresh or 5 oz (150 g) of dried horsetail in 2 gallons (10 l) of water for 24 hours. Then boil for a short time, allow to cool and strain. Dilute with five parts of water before use.

Tansy infusion

Tansy (*Tanacetum vulgaris*) is a yellow, daisy-like plant. Heat 10 oz (300 g) of fresh or 1 oz (30 g) of dried tansy in 2 gallons (10 l) of water, and use the resulting liquid undiluted against leaf-rolling sawfly and aphids.

Soap and alcohol solution

Dissolve 7 oz (200 g) of soft soap (available from chemists) in hot water, and dilute with 2 gallons (10 l) of water. Add 12 fl oz (0.3 l) of industrial alcohol and allow to cool. Use against aphids and red spider mite.

Interplanting these roses with salvias and ornamental grasses helps to keep them healthier.

Making a plant infusion

Soft soap solution

Dissolve 5-10 oz (150-300 g) soft soap in 2 gallons (10 l) of hot water, allow to cool and spray undiluted against aphids.

As prevention is always better than cure, roses should be given a regular natural feed to increase their resistance to mildew, rust and black spot. Good foliar feeds will make a good rose better, but will have little effect on a poor specimen.

The increasing popularity of patio rose gardens

The patio rose (see page 22) can quite aptly be described as the designer plant of the 20th century. With gardens decreasing in size, rose breeders were increasingly constrained in their enthusiasm to produce bigger and better roses, and searched for a formula to produce a perfect rose on a smaller scale.

The true patio rose is a plant some 18 in (45 cm) tall with correspondingly small flowers and foliage to match. Patio roses are highly suitable for use in modern garden design, and are in fact just as happy in small planting areas or where there are only a limited number of pots or troughs.

Patio Rose Garden, Dublin

Budding technique

Nearly all garden roses are produced by a process known as **budding**. This is the process whereby a **scion** or bud of one desirable variety is attached to the **cambium** of a rootstock from a wild rose. The cambium is the layer of dividing cells lying underneath the outer bark layer; without it the stem cannot grow.

Budding is necessary because the wild rose is more vigorous and usually more disease-resistant than the scion variety. The scion and rootstock then gradually grow together into a single plant.

Start by obtaining rootstocks from a specialist grower: these may be *Rosa canina* 'Inermis', *R.* × *laxa, R. multiflora* or another species or variety. It's also fairly easy to grow your own rootstocks by planting cuttings of the dog rose, *R. canina*, in autumn. The best time for budding is July or August. The budded rose won't actually flower until the following summer, but by the autumn you should at least be able to see whether or not the bud has taken.

Water the rootstock thoroughly for a couple of weeks before budding, so that the wood comes away more easily. You'll need a sharp knife, ideally a budding knife available from specialist suppliers. The buds should be ripe: not too

soft or too hard. If you can break the thorns off without damaging the wood, they'll be just about right. Ideally, you should use buds from a shoot which has just flowered. Remove the thorns and all the leaves except for a small piece of leaf stock 0.5-1 inch (1-2 cm) long: you'll need this to handle the bud, since its cut surface shouldn't be touched by human hands. Keep the buds in a plastic bag or a damp cloth until budding takes place.

Then remove enough soil to expose the neck of the rootstock, and wipe it carefully with a soft cloth. Take the shoot, and cut a short piece from the middle containing one bud. Place the knife 1 inch (2 cm) below the bud in the cambium, draw it through the cambium layer (i.e. between the wood and the bark) and then pull it out of the shoot again 1 inch (2 cm) above the bud. Throw away

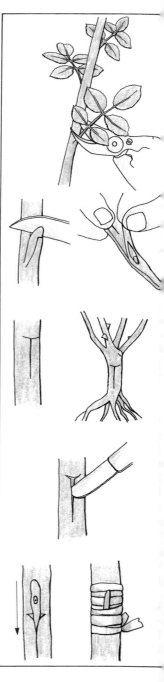

Budding: remove the leaves from the bud wood. Cut out the bud, and peel off the wood if it is too thick. Cut a 'T' in the rootstock (left: a standard; right: a rootstock). Pull away the wood and insert the bud, then tie it up with raffia.

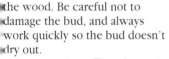

Hybrid tea rose 'Piccadilly'

the wood. Be careful not to damage the bud, and always work quickly so the bud doesn't dry out.

Now cut a long 'T' in the rootstock, lift the two flaps with the back of the budding knife and insert the bud downwards so that it sticks out at the top. Cut off this piece, and tie up the bud with raffia or a rubber patch so that only the tip of the bud is visible. Tie it tightly, but not too thickly; the raffia will rot and fall off after a few weeks. Finally, earth up the neck of the roots a little. After four weeks or so, check to see that the bud is still green and has thickened, in which case it has taken. The following spring, cut off the top of the rootstock about 1 inch (2 cm) above the T-shaped cut, and a shoot will grow from the bud. After three or four leaves have grown, pinch out the tip.

You'll need a rootstock with a long stem if you want to bud standard roses: in this case the bud is inserted into the stem at the desired height rather than at the neck.

Budding knives

You can buy a purpose-made budding knife with a projecting part on the back which is designed to make it easier to lift the flaps of the 'T' cut in the rootstock. The blade itself is specially shaped. However, you should find that any good-quality horticultural knife will do as well, provided it is kept really sharp.

Using stem cuttings

Roses can also be propagated by taking stem cuttings. It's relatively easy, and you can even use cuttings taken from bought cut flowers. These will grow in the same way as budded roses, but they tend to die off in a frost because they aren't as hardy. They won't last as long, either, even if they're in a protected position.

Hard-wood cuttings

The best roses to grow from these cuttings are miniature and ground-cover varieties, although the technique works perfectly well with other types. Cut a piece of stem about 12 in (30 cm) long after it has flowered. This doesn't necessarily have to include a shoot tip: it's possible, for example, to cut off a 24-inch (60-cm) long stem, cut it in half and plant both halves. Make sure it's this year's growth, not quite fully ripe, and contains three or four buds. Cut straight across the stem immediately below the bottom bud with a sharp knife or a razor blade. Dip the end first in water and then

Well worth propagating: the hybrid tea 'Blue Moon'

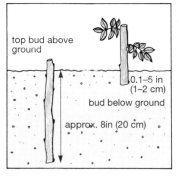

Propagation with hard-wood (left) and soft-wood (right) cuttings

n hormone rooting powder, remove all the lower leaves and plant the cuttings so that a finger-length piece (4 in/10 cm) with one bud on it is left above the surface.

The best position for growing cuttings is a special bed in a sheltered place in the garden, shaded from bright sunlight. Dig a narrow trench about as deep as the blade of a spade, and fill it with two parts garden soil, one part sand and three parts potting compost. Plant the cuttings, and keep them well watered but not too wet. The cuttings that root successfully can be moved to their permanent position 12 months later.

Soft-wood cuttings

Soft-wood cuttings can be grown in plastic pots, placed close together in a warm, damp atmosphere so that they don't dry out. Use potting compost or a similar growing medium suitable for cuttings, as this will help them to root quickly. The first roots will grow from the cut surface, and subsequent ones from near the buds which are buried.

If you want to bud roses, you should choose vigorous, long-lasting varieties. If grown in the proper soil, well fed and properly pruned, roses can last 30-35 years. A bright position in full sun with plenty of air is also essential for long life.

ROTY
Rose Of The Year

Breeding new roses is both exciting and laborious. The whole process from concept through hybridising (pollination), seed germination, and testing to the final selection of possible market winners can take as long as ten years. The final hurdle is the rose trials which are held in various parts of the world. In the UK, the Royal National Rose Society conducts what are considered the most stringent tests over a three-year period. The ultimate distinction is the award of a Gold Medal, while the very best is given the President's Trophy. Certificates of Merit and Trial Ground Awards to the runners-up are no mean achievements. Naming and marketing follows this examination.

The Rose Trade Association also conduct their own trials in collaboration with both growers and breeders. The culmination of this exercise is the annual award for Rose of the Year. It's usually announced at the world's finest flower show — the Chelsea Flower Show — and previous winners of the award include Royal William, Sweet Dream, Mountbatten and Melody Maker.

Botanical features of roses

Roses are shrubs, and like most other plants consist of roots, stems, leaves and flowers. Depending on the species, variety and class of rose, the stems or shoots form small bushes 8–12 in (20–30 cm) high or, in the case of climbing and rambling roses, stems several yards long. They have an upright, arching or spreading growth habit. The main stems grow from the bud union on the neck of the rose,

which is normally buried below ground. Suckers are shoots which grow from the rootstock.

Within the leaf **axils** (the angle formed by the leaf stalk and the stem to which it is joined) are buds which develop into new side shoots and make the plant bushier. Because the upper buds are thicker they're clearly visible, and will grow reasonably reliably, while the much smaller buds further

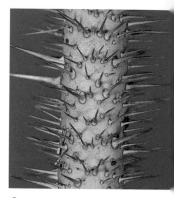

Some rose stems have very prominent thorns: this is R. rugosa.

down the plant are kept in reserve and known as **dormant buds**.

Thorns vary greatly in size, shape and colour. They may be sharp, blunt, thick or thin, and vary in colour through red, green, brown and yellow. Some roses, such as *R. sericea pteracantha*, have very large and attractive thorns; others, such as *R. pendulina*, are almost thornless.

As the rose is a deciduous plant, its leaves fall off in winter. They vary greatly in colour, size and shape, as do the flowers. Flower colours range from white through many different shades of yellow, pink and red to violet. Some have attractive combinations of two or more colours.

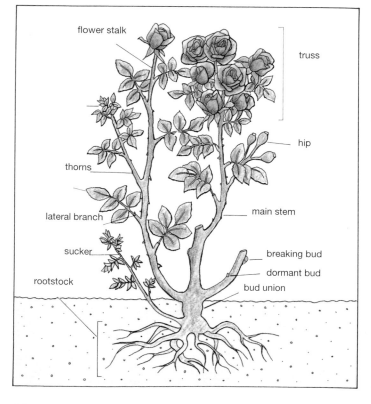

flower stalk

truss

hip

thorns

lateral branch

main stem

sucker

breaking bud

rootstock

dormant bud

bud union

Some of the botanical features of roses.

Rose hips

Hips are fruit, and like many other fruits they have a high carbohydrate content. They also contain large quantities of vitamin C, ranging from about 500 mg to 1,150 mg per 100 g. Lemons, commonly regarded as having a high vitamin C content, have only 60–100 mg per 100 g.

The rose species whose hips contain the most vitamin C are *R. pendulina* (1,100 mg per 100 g of fresh pulp), *R. rugosa* (940 mg), *R. villosa* (920 mg), *R. moyesii* (850 mg), and *R. rubrifolia* (820 mg). Rose hips also contain many other health-giving ingredients including vitamin K, niacin, vitamin A, essential oils, calcium, potassium, sodium, magnesium, iron, phosphorus and fruit acids.

Hips are not only very ornamental, they also have a high vitamin content and many uses in the kitchen.

Instances of roses in history and legend

Legend has it that the Greek poetess Sappho (6th century BC) was the first to describe the rose as Queen of the Flowers. But long before Sappho, roses were a mystical symbol in India: the most beautiful of all the goddesses, Lakshmi, was born from a rose. The Persian poet Hafiz (c. 1325–c. 1390) called the rose 'a beauty spot on the cheek of the world', and there's also an attractive Persian legend describing the coronation of the rose. The flowers asked God for a new ruler, as the sleepy Lotos would not keep watch at night. So God gave them the virginal white rose, with her protective thorns, as a princess regent. Muslims see the five petals of the old-fashioned single-flowered rose as the five secrets of God. They believe the rose was born from the sweat of the Prophet's brow when he ascended into heaven by night.

Ancient Greece and Rome

The ancient Greeks believed the precious white rose was created by the goddess Aphrodite from the blood of the dying Adonis.

Roman floor mosaic in the Vatican Museum, Rome

When she was wounded by a thorn, the rose became red as blood and fragrant as all the perfumes of Arabia.

In the more worldly atmosphere of ancient Rome the rose reached the apex of a career that already dated back several centuries. It was a symbol of extreme affluence and luxury. Roman emperors were reputed to dispose of unwanted subjects by inviting them to a banquet, then locking them in and showering them with rose petals until they were literally suffocated by opulence. This may be more legend than reality, but certainly Christianity banned the rose for 300 years afterwards as a pagan symbol.

Christianity and the rose

It was not until the early Middle Ages that the rose started to regain its popularity. It soon became a symbol of the Resurrection, and linked with the cult of the Virgin Mary. The round windows of Gothic cathedrals are known as 'rose windows', and rosaries were originally made from rose hips. Pope Hadrian V had roses placed over his confessional as a joyful symbol of silence. Perhaps the finest evidence of the religious symbolism of roses are the paintings executed by some of the great masters of the 15th century: Stefan Lochner's

Madonna in the rose arbour, Francesco Francia's *Mary in the rose grove* and Bernardino Luini's *Madonna and Child*. Even Napoleon had connections with the rose. His first wife Joséphine Beauharnais was the greatest rose patron of her time, and in 1798 Napoleon bought her Malmaison, where she assembled a collection of all known rose species. Malmaison became the world's greatest rose garden.

Martin Schongauer's Mary in the rose garden, *St Martin's Abbey, Colmar*

Roses for healing purposes

In the past, roses were regarded less as beautiful flowering plants and more as a medicine and a source of food. They were believed to be a panacea for many different illnesses, and not without reason: rose hips are full of vitamins and minerals. They have been widely used in the kitchen: they can be made into juice or a liqueur, stewed or made into jam, and the petals can also be used in salads and punches. Roses are also used extensively in cosmetic products such as perfumes, shampoos, massage oil, creams and rose-scented bath salts.

Bottling the scents of summer: rosewater

A selection of rose recipes

Rose-hip syrup

Ingredients to make 1½ pt (1 l) of syrup: 4½ lb (2 kg) rose hips, 2½-3½ pt (1.5-2 l) water, and 8-10 oz (250-300 g) granulated sugar.

Method: Remove the petals, stems and seeds from the hips and simmer over a moderate heat until soft but not pulpy. Filter the juice through very fine muslin. Stir in the sugar, boil for five minutes and pour into bottles while still hot. Rose-hip syrup only keeps for a week or so once the bottle has been opened, so it's best to use small bottles.

Rose-hip liqueur

Ingredients: about 1 lb (400-500 g) rose hips, 5 oz (150 g) granulated sugar, 1 bottle light spirit (e.g. vodka).

Method: Remove the flowers and stems from the hips, halve, and remove the 'blackhead' (or calyx), the hairs and the seeds. Wash the halved fruit well, leave to drain and place in a bottle. Then pour on the sugar and light spirit. Seal the bottle well and leave in a cool place for at least two months. Filter before use.

Rose-hip jam

Ingredients: 4 lb (2 kg) rose hips, and 2 lb (1 kg) granulated sugar.

Method: Wash the rose hips, remove the petals and stems, cut in half and remove the 'blackhead' (or calyx), the hairs and the seeds. Wash the halves, boil for 20 minutes just covered with water, and then purée. Allow to cool, mix with the sugar, bring to the boil and simmer for four minutes. Then pour into jars.

Rose-hip tea

Ingredients: 2-3 tablespoons dried and chopped rose hips, 2 pt (1 l) water.

Method: Place the dried hips in water and leave to stand for a few hours. Then boil for up to 10 minutes and strain.

Rose salad

Ingredients: 6-8 large roses, 2-3 lettuce hearts, 2 tbsp oil, 1-2 tbsp lemon juice, salt, 1 tsp honey, lemon balm, 1 small glass brandy, cinnamon.

Method: Remove the petals, throw away the damaged ones and wash the remainder. Shred the lettuce finely. Make a dressing from oil, lemon juice, salt, honey, brandy and finely chopped lemon balm. Mix this with the rose petals and lettuce and sprinkle with cinnamon.

Rose punch

Ingredients (serves 10): 1 bottle white wine, 1 bottle red wine, 1 bottle sparkling wine or mineral water, 4½ fl oz (125 ml) brandy or Grand Marnier, 10 fragrant rose petals (which must not have been sprayed).

Method: Place the petals in the punch bowl, pour the brandy over them and leave covered for an hour. Then add the wine, remove the petals after half an hour and pour on the chilled sparkling wine or mineral water. Place a fresh rose petal in each glass, pour the punch over it and serve with the petal floating in it.

Rose hips can be bottled in the same way as strawberries or cherries.

Various rose arrangements

Vases and bouquets

Roses, especially hybrid teas, are one of the most popular and beautiful cut flowers. Some varieties make particularly good cut flowers, partly because of their colour and fragrance, and partly because they have long, straight stems. But don't limit yourself to hybrid teas: other types of rose work just as well in a vase. Modern shrub roses, for example, are particularly long-lasting when cut, and in the right conditions they'll continue to look fresh for a week or more. Summer-flowering shrub roses — such as the Golden Rose of China (*Rosa hugonis*), with its small, single golden-yellow flowers — look particularly attractive in a vase.

Cut the roses when the buds are starting to show some colour. Remove all the leaves on the lower third of the stem, and cut so the stem is as long as possible. The beautifully fragrant moss roses (*R. centifolia muscosa*) shouldn't be cut until the flower is about to open. Closed buds will not open. Moss roses look superb in combination with delphiniums or marguerites. Unfortunately, like other double-flowered shrub roses, they won't last very long; the same goes for other old roses, and for New English roses. Floribundas will last longer if all unripe buds are cut off. Unlike with hybrid teas, the main bud (i.e. the one which flowers first) should be removed, and the stems shouldn't be cut until most of the lateral buds have flowered.

Making cut roses last longer

There are a number of rules to follow if you want to make sure that cut roses of all kinds last as long as possible. First, keep the vase or container scrupulously

Hang roses upside down to dry.

lean. Before you arrange the roses in the vase, remove a few leaves from the flower stalks to reduce evaporation, and take off all the leaves that would otherwise be submerged. Always cut the stems diagonally, with a sharp knife, and place them in water immediately. Use chrysal to remove toxins from the water and feed the flowers. Cut off the very ends of the stems whenever you change the water. There's no need to change the water if you have added chrysal. Instead, keep an eye on the depth of the water, and add water and cut flower food regularly. Roses dislike draughts and direct sunlight, and will also last longer if they're always kept in a cool place at night.

Using roses as dried flowers

There are various ways of drying roses so they can be used in dried flower and various other arrangements.

The simplest is to tie the stems together in bundles of about ten to twenty using string or raffia (but not elastic bands) and hang them upside down in a dry, well-ventilated and bright position. As the stems shrink, you'll probably have to tighten the strings a couple of times.

Roses are also ideal for flower arrangements

The warmer the room, the faster the roses will dry. Sometimes you'll need to provide some extra heat, perhaps by hanging the roses above a cooker while you're cooking.

Useful addresses

If you're a rose-lover, summer will be your busiest time of year. When you're not tending your own roses, you should be out at garden centres, specialist rose growers and rose gardens admiring other people's. Take a notepad with you to write down the names of varieties that particularly take your fancy. Most are fairly easy to obtain, and there has been a resurgence in the propagation and sale of old roses which narrowly escaped being consigned to oblivion.

Rose gardens in the United Kingdom

Devon Rosemoor (RHS), Torrington
Essex Hyde Hall (RHS), Rettendon
Gloucestershire Kiftsgate Court, Chipping Campden
Hampshire Mottisfont Abbey, Romsey
Hertfordshire Garden of the Royal National Rose Society, St Albans
Kent Sissinghurst Castle, Sissinghurst
London Queen Mary's Garden, Regent's Park
Norfolk Mannington Hall, Saxthorpe
North Yorkshire Castle Howard
Surrey Wisley Gardens (RHS), Woking
Northern Ireland Sir Thomas and Lady Dixon Park, Belfast

Rose gardens in continental Europe

Austria Austrian Rose Garden, Baden, near Vienna; Botanic Garden and Arboretum, Linz; Donaupark and Kurpark Oberlaa, Vienna.
Belgium Queen Astrid Park, Ghent; West Flanders Rose Garden, Kortrijk.
Denmark University Botanic Garden, Copenhagen; Valbyparken, Copenhagen.

France La Roseraie du Parc Nicolas, Chalon-sur-Saône; Parc de la Tête d'Or, Lyon; Roseraie du Parc Florëal, Orlëans; L'Haÿ-les-Roses, Paris; Parc de Bagatelle, Paris.
Germany Baden-Baden; Insel Mainau, Bodensee; Westfalenpark, Dortmund; Sangerhausen; Zweibrücken.
Italy Villa Grimaldi, Genoa; Villa Reale, Monza; Municipal Rose Garden, Rome.
Netherlands Westbroekpark, The Hague; Winschoten Rose Garden.
Spain Rosaleda Ramon Ortiz,

Parque del Oeste, Madrid;
Parque del Retiro, Madrid.
Switzerland Rose Garden,
Dottikon; Parc la Grange,
Geneva; Rapperswil Rose
Gardens.

Rose growers and mail order suppliers

David Austin Roses, Bowling
Green Lane, Albrighton,
Wolverhampton
Peter Beales Roses, London
Road, Attleborough, **Norfolk**

Worth a detour: Roseraie de l'Haÿ-les-Roses, south-east of Paris.

Cants of Colchester, Nyland
Road, Colchester, **Essex**
James Cocker & Sons,
Whitmyers, Lang Stracht,
Aberdeen
Fryers Nurseries Ltd,
Manchester Road, Knutsford,
Cheshire
Gandy's Roses, North Kilworth,
Lutterworth, **Leicestershire**
R. Harkness & Co. Ltd, The Rose
Gardens, Cambridge Road,
Hitchin, **Hertfordshire**
Hill Park Nurseries, Kingston
Bypass, Surbiton, **Surrey**
C. & K. Jones, Golden Fields
Nursery, Barrow Lane, Tarvin,
Cheshire
E. B. le Grice (Roses) Ltd,
Norwich Road, North Walsham,
Norfolk
Mattock's Roses, Nuneham
Courtenay, **Oxford**
John Sanday (Roses) Ltd, Over
Lane, Almondsbury, **Bristol**
Stydd Nursery, Stoneygate Lane,
Ribchester, Preston, **Lancs**
Warley Rose Gardens Ltd, Great
Worsley, Brentwood, **Essex**

Rose accessories

Most reputable garden centres
and plant information bureaux
stock a wide range of horticultural sundries such as rose
arches, trellises, pyramids, fertilisers, soil testing kits and
bowls.

Rose societies

Many countries have rose
societies. As well as holding
lectures and rose shows they
publish definitive literature, and
you'll find them extremely
friendly . The World Federation

of Rose Societies holds frequent
conferences.

United Kingdom
The Royal National Rose Society
Chiswell Green, St Albans,
Hertfordshire AL2 3NR
The Royal Horticultural Society,
80 Vincent Square, London
SW1P 2PE
The Rose Society of Northern
Ireland, 10 Eastleigh Drive,
Belfast BT4 3DX

Australia
The National Rose Society of
Australia, 271B Belmore Road,
North Balwyn, Victoria 3104

Austria
Österreichische, Gartenbau-
gesellschaft, Parkring 12/III 1,
A-1010 Vienna 1

Switzerland
Dietrich Woessner,
Nelkenstrasse 26, CH-8212
Neuhausen

France
Sociètè Française des Roses, 6
Rue J. B. Couty, 69009 Lyon

Germany
Verein Deutscher Rosenfreunde
eV, Walderseestrasse 14, 7570
Baden-Baden

Useful publications

The British Rose Growers'
Association publishes *Find that
Rose* annually; copies may be
obtained from: 303 Mile End
Road, Colchester, Essex
CO4 5EA
   A similar international list can
be obtained from: Peter
Schneider, PO Box 16035,
Rocky River, OH 441166, USA.

Index